THE TOFOO Co. Cookbook

THE TofOO co.
Cookbook

EBURY
PRESS

CONTENTS

1
First Thing
14

2
Baps & Wraps
30

3
Soups & Salads
68

4
Delicious Dinners

5
A Bit on the Side

WELCOME TO THE TOFOO COOKBOOK!

Tofu has long been one of the most unloved and misunderstood foods. It would seem 'tofuphobia' takes many forms: some assume it's just for veggies, others are put off by memories of a bad Chinese meal and most are just perplexed with what do with that funny-looking white block. Back in 2016, we decided it was time to show the world just how brilliant tofu can be. No longer to be pushed away into a dark corner or to be the punchline to bad jokes about vegan cooking, it was time to bring great-tasting tofu to the masses!

Building a great business was always a dream of ours and we set our hearts on developing a brand that celebrated all the wonderful things you can do with this amazing ingredient. We came across a small artisan tofu business in Malton, North Yorkshire, run by a tofu lover who wanted to retire, and we could see real potential! We organised a visit to the factory and, upon trying the product, we just knew this was the start of something good – we had never tasted tofu like this – it was different, it was special, it was Tofoo.

Right from the very beginning, we knew we wanted The Tofoo Co. to represent not only amazing tofu, but all the values that are important to us, like great teamwork, sustainability, ethical sourcing, quality ingredients and great craftsmanship.

The Tofoo Co. has grown quickly but continues to focus on that amazing product we first discovered in Malton, and we're proud to be launching our very own Tofoo cookbook to show you how easy it is to transform one block of Tofoo into hundreds of different and delicious dishes. So, if you were once that person who turned their nose up at tofu, we urge you to give Tofoo a go. And we hope you will join us in saying: 'I love Tofoo!'

Dave Knibbs & Lydia Smith
Owners & Founders of The Tofoo Co.

Take everything you know about tofu and file it under 'things I used to think that turned out to be wrong'.

*Actually, not ALL tofu, just ours

Tofoo's not the soggy, tasteless stuff you might be thinking of, and we're on a mission to show the world that tofu is really rather brilliant.*

Tofu's a super healthy, super versatile plant-based protein and its subtle flavour allows it to be a total taste chameleon, taking on the flavour of any dish it goes in. But what makes Tofoo any different to your average block of tofu? Well, we'll tell you ...

The Tofoo Co. is an independent family business in Malton, North Yorkshire run by husband-and-wife team David Knibbs and Lydia Smith. Every block of our humble Tofoo is lovingly handmade to a traditional Japanese recipe. Our organic Naked Tofoo is made with just three natural ingredients – yes, three! Water, soya beans and nigari (a natural extract made from seawater). And, here at The Tofoo Co. HQ we have a super sourcing policy so only the finest beans will make it through our front door. Our soya beans have to be from a sustainable source, must always be organic, and of course GM-free too. This is our bean guarantee.

HOW IS TOFOO MADE?

Our soya beans are first soaked for at least 24 hours. After this they are blended with water before separating out the soya milk from the pulp. The milk is then heated and mixed with nigari and left to sit, separating out the curds and whey. The bean curd is scooped by our Tofoo makers into muslin-cloth-lined setting boxes, pressed and left to rest to remove any extra water before cutting into Tofoo-sized blocks. Our Tofoo is made in small batches, which is why you find natural variation in its appearance, but always the same great taste and texture.

PREPARING AND COOKING TOFOO

The best thing about our tofu? You don't need to press it! Tofoo is firm enough without any meddling – just drain, chop, cook and enjoy. Tofoo can also be enjoyed hot or cold, so it's perfect for anything from stir-fries to salads.

HOW TO GET THE BEST OUT OF TOFOO

There's about a million ways to prepare our tofu. You can slice it, dice it, cut it into strips – thick, thin, long, short – triangles or even crumble or grate it. You can also rip it, giving extra surface area for a marinade to seep in or for the edges to get extra crunchy. There's almost nothing you can't do with Tofoo.

On the next page are a few tips and techniques to prepare and cook Tofoo. Master these and the world is your Tofoo oyster.

TOP TIPS FOR TASTY TOFOO

1 SEASON

Praise be to seasoning and all hail the taste! Give Tofoo as much flavouring as you like. It loves herbs, spice and strong flavours. Rub Tofoo with seasoning for maximum impact.

2 MARINADE

Tofoo loves a marinade to feed its flavour. Hot chilli, sesame and soy sauce are a brilliant starting point. Citrus flavours such as lemon, lime or orange, or a vinegar will give your marinade freshness and sharpness. Want to go smoky? Try barbecue sauce, harissa or smoked paprika. Avoid using too much oil in the marinade as it can prevent the flavours soaking into the Tofoo. The longer you marinate Tofoo, the better.

3 CRISP

Give Tofoo some added crispiness with a good dusting of flour or cornflour before it goes into a super-hot frying pan. Cut or rip Tofoo into pieces and dust in cornflour, giving it a good coating. Add flavour by adding some seasoning or spice to the cornflour.

4 CRUNCH

Crunchy and soft – the best combination. Give Tofoo a crispier, crunchier bite by coating it in breadcrumbs. Use shop-bought breadcrumbs or even make your own with stale bread. Season the crumbs or use plain; perfect for Tofoo katsu, Tofoo goujons fillets or nuggets. If you want to go for the double whammy – marinate your Tofoo and then coat in breadcrumbs.

5 SCRAMBLE

Tofoo scramble is a really useful dish to master. Crumble a Naked Tofoo block into a bowl. Add milk and ground turmeric, season and combine well. In a pan, add a splash of oil and a knob of the spread of your choice and bring to a high heat, add the scrambled Tofoo mix and stir until hot.

6 OIL

Olive oil is good for lots of things, but not for frying Tofoo. It just can't handle the heat you'll need in your pan. Sunflower is a great staple, or, for oils to make Tofoo crispier with added flavour, try sesame or coconut oil instead.

7 FRY

When frying Tofoo, heat the oil in a pan and get it as hot as you can. Fry the Tofoo, dusted or plain, for about 5 minutes or until golden brown all over. Add the sauce and vegetables as per the recipe.

8 BAKE

When baking, remember to preheat the oven. Tofoo likes it at 200°C/180°C fan/400°F/gas mark 6. Toss the Tofoo in oil and place in a single layer on a baking sheet lined with baking paper. If you are going for extra crunch, sprinkle over a little cornflour. Cook for 20 minutes, turning once or twice or until golden brown and crisp.

9 STORE

Tofoo should be kept refrigerated below 5°C, and you should always check the use by on the side of pack of the Tofoo. Once opened, place any remaining Tofoo in water in an airtight container and use within 48 hours.

10 FREEZE

Tofoo is suitable for freezing, but this can change its texture. You can also freeze Tofoo in a meal after cooking, so get batch cooking!

Tofoo loves flavour, so stock up on these essentials to get the best out of your block:

☐ Ground turmeric

☐ Paprika – sweet, hot or smoked

☐ Ground cumin

☐ Chilli flakes and powder

☐ Chinese 5 spice

☐ Soy sauce

☐ Maple syrup

☐ Vinegar – red wine, white wine, apple cider or rice

☐ Sesame oil – toasted and pure

☐ Miso paste

☐ Sriracha sauce

☐ Tomato ketchup

☐ Garlic – fresh, paste or powder

☐ Ginger – fresh or paste

☐ Mint – fresh and dried

☐ Coriander – fresh

☐ Lemons and limes

☐ Nutritional yeast

☐ Sea salt

☐ Ground black pepper

☐ Cornflour ← It may not aid the flavour but is ESSENTIAL for that dreamy crunch!

MAKE IT VEGAN

All of the recipes throughout the book can be made vegan friendly by using your choice of vegan alternative for dairy products.

1
First Thing

SCRAMBLED TOFOO & AVOCADO BREAKFAST BAGEL

Some food combinations are just perfect. Tofoo, avocado and hot sauce are a match made in breakfast heaven.

Serves: **2**
Preparation: **20 MINUTES**
Cooking: **4 MINUTES**

GET THIS STUFF

½ x 280g pack Naked
   Tofoo, drained, dried
   and crumbled
¼ tsp ground turmeric
2 tbsp milk of your choice
½ ripe avocado
juice of ½ lemon
pinch of freshly ground
   black pepper
pinch of chilli flakes
1 tbsp olive oil
2 sesame seed bagels,
   halved and toasted
a few sprigs of dill,
   chopped
drizzle of sriracha
handful of watercress,
   washed
sea salt and freshly ground
   black pepper

DO THIS STUFF

For the scrambled Tofoo, place the crumbled Tofoo in a bowl and add the turmeric and milk. Season generously and mix well. Set aside until ready to cook.

In a bowl, smash the avocado with a fork, adding the lemon juice, pepper and chilli flakes.

Heat the oil in a frying pan, add the Tofoo and cook over a medium heat for 4 minutes, stirring regularly, until the Tofoo colours and there are a few delicious crispy bits.

Spread the avocado over the base of the toasted bagels, top with the scrambled Tofoo, dill, a drizzle of sriracha and a pile of watercress. Season generously with black pepper. Finish with the bagel tops. Eat immediately.

WHY NOT TRY:

Using sweet chilli sauce if sriracha is too hot for you first thing in the morning.

TOFOO BREAKFAST MUFFIN

This delicious savoury breakfast muffin is a brilliant break from boring old cereal and will set you up with all the energy you need for the day ahead.

GET THIS STUFF

1 x 280g pack Naked Tofoo, drained and dried
¼ tsp ground turmeric
4 portobello mushrooms
2 tbsp sunflower oil
1 beef tomato, sliced into four
4 breakfast muffins
1–2 tbsp butter
tomato ketchup
sea salt and freshly ground black pepper

DO THIS STUFF

Preheat the oven to 180°C/160°C fan/350°F/gas mark 4.

Slice the Tofoo along the longer side into four thick slices. Cut each slice into a 6cm round, either using a cutter or cutting freehand.

Place the Tofoo in a shallow dish. Sprinkle over half the turmeric, turn over and sprinkle with the remaining turmeric. If you do not mind having yellow fingers, you can rub the turmeric into the Tofoo. Leave to stand for 30 minutes or as long as you have.

Wipe the portobello mushrooms and remove the stalks.

Heat 1 tablespoon of oil in a large frying pan over a medium heat. Place the Tofoo slices in the pan and cook for 5 minutes, then carefully turn over with a fish slice and cook for a further 4 minutes.

Place the Tofoo on a baking tray and place in the oven while you cook the tomato and mushrooms.

Wipe the frying pan clean and add the remaining oil. Add the sliced beef tomato and the portobello mushroom, gill side down.

Serves: **4**
Preparation: **10 MINUTES**
Marinating: **30 MINUTES**
Cooking: **25 MINUTES**

Cook for about 5 minutes, or until the tomato and mushrooms are just beginning to colour. Carefully turn over and cook for a further 4 minutes until brown. Place on the tray with the Tofoo while you prepare the muffins.

Cut the muffins in half and toast until golden brown. Spread each half with the butter.

Layer the mushroom, tomato and finally the Tofoo on one half of the toasted muffins. Add a good squirt of tomato ketchup and top with the other half of the muffins. Serve immediately.

Not a fan of ketchup? Try brown sauce instead!

WHY NOT TRY:

- Adding a slice of cheese and Tofoo bacon (see page 21).
- Serving in a floury bap instead.

TOFOO FULL ENGLISH BREAKFAST

Everyone knows the weekend doesn't start until you've had a great big fry-up, whether you're recovering from a heavy Friday night or not! Making a Full English requires a bit of juggling to get everything ready at once, but practice makes perfect and it's well worth it.

Serves: **4**
Preparation: **25 MINUTES**
Marinating: **30 MINUTES**
Cooking: **25 MINUTES**

GET THIS STUFF

1 x 225g pack Smoked Tofoo, drained, dried and thinly sliced
8 sausages
2 tomatoes, halved
2 tbsp olive oil
1 x 415g can baked beans
8 chestnut mushrooms, wiped and sliced
butter
4 slices of bread
tomato ketchup or brown sauce (optional)

For the Tofoo bacon marinade
75ml light soy sauce
1 tbsp brown sauce
1 tbsp tomato ketchup
1 tbsp maple syrup
½ tbsp white miso paste
pinch of freshly ground black pepper

DO THIS STUFF

For the Tofoo bacon, place the Tofoo slices into a shallow bowl. Whisk together the marinade ingredients and add to the sliced Tofoo. Cover and marinate for 30 minutes or for as long as possible. You can prep this the night before and let it soak in all the flavours overnight in the fridge.

To make the scrambled Tofoo, place the crumbled Tofoo in a bowl and add the turmeric, cayenne pepper and milk. Season generously and mix well. Set aside until ready to cook.

Preheat the oven to 180°C/160°C fan/350°F/gas mark 4. Line two trays with baking paper.

On one tray, place the sausages and tomatoes and brush with a little olive oil. On the other tray, lay out the Tofoo bacon. Bake the Tofoo bacon for 25 minutes, turning and brushing with the marinade halfway through cooking. Bake the sausages and tomatoes for 20 minutes or until the tomatoes are soft and the sausages are browned.

Ingredients & method continued on the next page

Still hungry? Add a hash brown or a grilled whole mushroom.

For the scrambled Tofoo
1 x 280g pack Naked Tofoo, drained, dried and crumbled
½ tsp ground turmeric
¼ tsp cayenne pepper
3 tbsp milk, of your choice
sea salt and freshly ground black pepper

Meanwhile, add a splash of olive oil and a knob of butter to a pan over a medium heat, then add the scrambled Tofoo and cook for 4–6 minutes, stirring occasionally, until the Tofoo colours and there are a few delicious crispy bits.

Add a splash of olive oil and a knob of butter to a small frying pan over a medium–high heat and fry the mushrooms for 4 minutes until golden brown.

Warm the baked beans in a pan over a medium heat. Keep warm until ready to serve.

Toast the bread, and butter while hot. Divide the sausages, tomatoes, Tofoo bacon, scrambled Tofoo, mushrooms, baked beans and toast between four plates. Serve immediately with a dollop of tomato ketchup or brown sauce.

TOFOO BREAKFAST BURRITOS

This is a perfect weekend brunch recipe. Want to load up your burrito? Add avocado, shredded red cabbage, spinach or cheese for a chunkier wrap.

Serves: **4**
Preparation: **20 MINUTES**
Cooking: **15 MINUTES**

GET THIS STUFF

300g brown rice
1 x 400g can kidney beans,
   drained and rinsed
4 tbsp olive oil
2 x 225g packs Smoked
   Tofoo, drained, dried
   and crumbled
1 garlic clove, crushed
½ tsp ground turmeric
pinch of paprika
4 wholemeal tortillas
sea salt and freshly ground
   black pepper
hot sauce, to serve
1 lime, cut into wedges,
   to serve

For the tomato salsa
1 red onion, diced
6 tomatoes, diced
2 spring onions, chopped
bunch of coriander,
   roughly chopped
juice of 1 lime
drizzle of olive oil

DO THIS STUFF

For the tomato salsa, mix the red onion, tomatoes and spring onions together in a bowl. Add the coriander, lime juice and a drizzle of olive oil. Stir and refrigerate until ready to serve.

Bring a large pan of salted water to the boil. Rinse the rice in a sieve under running water to remove any excess starch. Add the rice to the boiling water, reduce the heat and boil, uncovered, for 30 minutes. After 25 minutes, add the kidney beans.

Meanwhile, heat 1 tbsp olive oil in a large frying pan and add the crumbled Tofoo, stirring while cooking. Once the Tofoo starts to brown, add the garlic, turmeric, paprika and a good grinding of salt and pepper. Cook for a further 5 minutes or until the garlic has softened and the Tofoo is golden brown.

Once the rice is cooked, remove the pan from the heat. Drain, return to the pan and mash up the rice and beans together. Do not mash into a paste, just until they are bashed up a bit. Season with salt.

Continued on the next page

To assemble a burrito, lay out a tortilla wrap. Fill the centre with the rice mix, top with some Tofoo and tomato salsa. Heat the remining oil in a large frying pan. Wrap up the burrito and place in the frying pan. Cook for about 3 minutes on each side until brown and crisp, then remove from the pan. Repeat with the remaining wraps and filling.

Serve with some hot sauce and lime wedges. Tuck in!

WHY NOT TRY:

Using leftover rice or even a pouch of microwave rice, if easier.

TOFOO SCRAMBLE BAGEL
with smoked salmon

Vegan smoked salmon is available online, in supermarkets or specialist stores, or why not try and make your own with carrots?

Serves: **2**
Preparation: **15 MINUTES**
Cooking: **10-15 MINUTES**

GET THIS STUFF

2 bagels, halved
1 x 113g pack smoked
   salmon or lox
1 tsp fresh dill
2 tbsp capers, drained
½ small red onion,
   thinly sliced

For the scrambled Tofoo
100ml milk of your choice
2 tbsp nutritional yeast
1 garlic clove, crushed
½ tsp Dijon mustard
¼ tsp ground turmeric
pinch of ground cumin
1 tbsp olive oil
2 spring onions, chopped
½ x 280g pack Naked
   Tofoo, drained, dried
   and crumbled
sea salt and freshly ground
   black pepper

DO THIS STUFF

In a small bowl, whisk together the milk, nutritional yeast, garlic, mustard, turmeric, cumin and ½ teaspoon of salt. Set aside.

Heat the olive oil in a large frying pan over a medium heat. Add the spring onions and cook for about 3 minutes or until soft. Stir in the Tofoo and cook for 3–5 minutes until the Tofoo is thoroughly heated. Reduce the heat to low and stir in the milk mixture. Cook for 3 minutes, stirring occasionally, until most of the milk has evaporated and you are left with a thick, glossy sauce coating the scrambled Tofoo. Season to taste with more salt and freshly ground black pepper.

When ready to serve, toast the bagels.

Spoon the scrambled Tofoo on to the bagels and top with the smoked salmon. Sprinkle with the dill, capers and red onion. Season generously and serve.

Make it a New York-style bagel by adding pickled radish or a sliced gherkin

WHY NOT TRY:

Adding capers and dill to the scrambled egg and serving on toast.

SPICY SCRAMBLED TOFOO BREAKFAST TACOS

Feeling the heat? Add more spice or add another chilli to the mix if you think you can handle it ...

Serves: **2**
Preparation: **20 MINUTES**
Cooking: **20 MINUTES**

GET THIS STUFF

75ml milk of your choice
1 tbsp nutritional yeast
½ tsp Dijon mustard
¼ tsp ground turmeric
chilli flakes, to taste
1 tbsp vegetable oil
1 green chilli, deseeded
    and finely chopped
1 small onion, finely
    chopped
1 small garlic clove, chopped
1 medium tomato, chopped
70g sweetcorn, drained
    or defrosted
½ x 280g pack Naked
    Tofoo, drained, dried
    and crumbled
4 small corn tortillas
½ ripe avocado, sliced
sea salt and freshly ground
    black pepper

To serve
fresh coriander leaves
hot sauce (optional)

DO THIS STUFF

In a small bowl, whisk together the milk, nutritional yeast, mustard, turmeric, chilli flakes and ½ teaspoon of salt. Set aside.

Heat the oil in a non-stick frying pan. Add the chilli and onion and cook for 3–4 minutes until beginning to soften and colour round the edges. Add the garlic and cook for 30–40 seconds. Add the tomato and sweetcorn and season well. Cook over a medium heat for 3–4 minutes or until the tomato has just softened.

Add the Tofoo and cook for 3–5 minutes until the Tofoo is thoroughly heated. Reduce the heat to low and stir in the milk mixture. Cook for 3 minutes, stirring occasionally, until most of the milk has evaporated and you are left with a thick, glossy sauce coating the scrambled Tofoo. Season to taste with more salt and freshly ground black pepper.

Following the pack instructions, warm the tortillas in the microwave. Spoon the scrambled Tofoo into the middle of each tortilla. Top with sliced avocado and sprinkle over the coriander leaves. Drizzle over some hot sauce if you like. Fold the tortillas in half and serve hot.

WHY NOT TRY:

Adding garam masala and extra cumin to the milk and serving with naan.

TOFOO SHAKSHUKA

This is a brunch classic and a delicious Middle Eastern dish with an added twist of harissa spice mix. Traditionally, this dish is served for breakfast, but it's delicious enough to eat at any time of the day.

Serves: **4**
Preparation: **15 MINUTES**
Cooking: **40 MINUTES**

GET THIS STUFF

1 x 225g pack Smoked Tofoo, drained and dried
2 tbsp cornflour
2 tsp paprika
4 tbsp sunflower oil
1 onion, sliced
1 large red pepper, deseeded and sliced
1 large yellow pepper, deseeded and sliced
3 garlic cloves, finely chopped
2 tbsp harissa paste
2 x 400g cans chopped tomatoes
1 tbsp tomato purée
1 tsp caster sugar
handful of coriander, roughly chopped
sea salt and freshly ground black pepper

To serve
flatbreads

DO THIS STUFF

Slice the Tofoo into four pieces and cut each slice into a triangle. You will have eight triangles. Dry each slice with kitchen paper. Mix together the cornflour and paprika. Place the Tofoo into a shallow bowl and coat in the paprika cornflour.

Heat half the oil in a large frying pan, add the Tofoo and cook for 2–3 minutes on each side until the Tofoo is golden brown and crunchy. Remove from the frying pan and set aside.

Add the remaining oil and the onion to the pan and cook for 8–10 minutes, or until the onions start to soften and colour. Add the peppers and cook for 4–6 minutes until soft, then stir in the garlic and the harissa paste. Cook for a further couple of minutes.

Add the tomatoes, tomato purée and sugar, and bring to the boil. Reduce the heat and simmer for 15 minutes. Taste and season.

Slide the crispy Tofoo into the pan, semi-submerging it in the sauce. Cook for a further 10 minutes so the Tofoo absorbs the flavours. Sprinkle with coriander and serve with a stack of flatbreads to mop up the delicious juices.

WHY NOT TRY:

Adding chopped courgettes or spinach to the mix.

2
Baps & Wraps

FAUX TOFOO EGG & CRESS SANDWICH

This sandwich is so quick to make with no cooking required. Ideal for an everyday packed lunch and a picnic staple.

Serves: **2**

Preparation: **10 MINUTES**

GET THIS STUFF

1 x 280g pack Naked Tofoo, drained and dried
¼ tsp ground turmeric
pinch of cayenne pepper
2 tbsp mayonnaise
butter
1 punnet of cress, snipped
4 thick slices of white bloomer, wholemeal or sourdough bread
sea salt and freshly ground black pepper

DO THIS STUFF

In a bowl, crumble the Tofoo into small pieces. Sprinkle in the turmeric and cayenne, and season generously with salt and black pepper. Mix well and add the mayonnaise little by little until bound together. Add half the snipped cress and gently fold in.

Butter the bread and put half of the Tofoo mix on to two of the slices, sprinkle with the remaining cress and top with the remaining slices of bread. Cut each sandwich in half and serve.

Makes a lovely lunch!

WHY NOT TRY:

Giving this sandwich an extra boost by replacing the cress with micro greens or chopped watercress.

TOFOO TOASTIES THREE WAYS

Sometimes nothing can beat a good toastie – the perfect cosy comfort food. If you have a toastie maker, just chuck these bad boys in there for an even quicker lunch!

CRISPY TOFOO, BRIE & CRANBERRY TOASTIE

Serves: **1**
Preparation: **5 MINUTES**
Cooking: **15 MINUTES**

GET THIS STUFF

- ¼ x 280g pack Naked Tofoo, drained, dried and cut into 4 slices
- 1 tbsp cornflour
- 1 tbsp sunflower oil
- 2 slices of white bread, toasted on one side
- 4 slices of Brie
- 2 tbsp cranberry sauce

DO THIS STUFF

Preheat the oven to 180°C/160°C fan/350°F/gas mark 4. Preheat the grill to medium.

Dry each slice of Tofoo. Put the cornflour in a bowl, add the Tofoo and coat completely in the cornflour. Heat 1cm of oil in a frying pan over a medium heat. Add the floured Tofoo slices and cook for 4 minutes on each side. Remove from the oil and leave to cool on a few sheets of kitchen paper.

Place the bread, toasted side up, on a board and layer up the sliced Brie, crispy Tofoo and cranberry sauce, then top with the second bit of bread, toasted side down, and place on a baking tray.

Toast the toastie top under a hot grill for 1 minute. Keep an eye on your toastie and, once golden, turn the toastie upside down and toast the other side for a further minute while, once again, keeping a sharp eye on your toastie. Toast until golden.

Now place the tray in the oven and bake for 12 minutes or until the cheese is fully melted. Remove the toastie from the tray, cut in half or into quarters and serve.

SMOKED TOFOO TOASTIE WITH RED LEICESTER & SPRING ONION

Serves: **1**
Preparation: **5 MINUTES**
Cooking: **15 MINUTES**

GET THIS STUFF

½ x 225g pack Smoked Tofoo, drained, dried and cut into 6 slices
1 tbsp sunflower oil
2 slices of brown bread, toasted on one side
3 slices of Red Leicester
2 tbsp spring onions, chopped

For the glaze
2 tbsp maple syrup
2 tbsp dark soy sauce
1 tsp rice wine vinegar

DO THIS STUFF

Preheat the oven to 180°C/160°C fan/350°F/gas mark 4. Preheat the grill to medium.

For the glaze, mix together the maple syrup, soy sauce and rice wine vinegar.

On the hob, heat a griddle pan to a medium–high heat, brush the sliced Tofoo with the oil and place in the hot griddle pan for 2 minutes. Turn each piece 45 degrees and cook for a further 2 minutes. Turn each piece over and repeat.

Pour the glaze over the Tofoo and turn each piece again so the slices are coated. Remove from the heat.

Place the Red Leicester on the toasted side of a slice of bread, then layer with the glazed Tofoo and spring onions. Top with the other slice of bread, toasted side down, and put on a baking tray.

Toast the toastie top under a hot grill for 1 minute. Keep an eye on your toastie and, once golden, turn the toastie upside down and toast the other side for a further minute while, once again, keeping a sharp eye on your toastie. Toast until golden.

Now place the tray in the oven and bake for 12 minutes or until the cheese is fully melted. Remove the toastie from the tray, cut in half or into quarters and serve.

TOFOO BACON, CHEDDAR & SPINACH TOASTIE

Serves: **1**
Preparation: **5 MINUTES**
Cooking: **18 MINUTES**

GET THIS STUFF

50g spinach
6 slices of Smoked Tofoo bacon (see page 21)
2 slices of white bread, toasted on one side
3 slices of Cheddar cheese

DO THIS STUFF

Preheat the oven to 180°C/160°C fan/350°F/gas mark 4. Preheat the grill to medium.

In a saucepan, bring 100ml water to the boil, add the spinach and stir for 3 minutes until just wilted. Drain on a clean tea towel and pat dry.

Place the Tofoo bacon, Cheddar cheese and wilted spinach on the toasted side of a slice of bread. Top with the other slice, toasted side down, and place on a baking tray.

Toast the toastie top under a hot grill for 1 minute. Keep an eye on your toastie and, once golden, turn the toastie upside down and toast the other side for a further minute while, once again, keeping a sharp eye on your toastie. Toast until golden.

Now place the tray in the oven and bake for 12 minutes or until the cheese is fully melted. Remove the toastie from the tray, cut in half or into quarters and serve.

TO MAKE IN A TOASTIE MAKER

Heat the sandwich toaster until the desired temperature is reached. Brush the plates with oil, or butter the untoasted side of the bread. Place one piece of bread on each of the bottom plates (butter side down), and pile on the filling of choice, leaving a small distance from the crust. Place another slice of bread on top to form a sandwich (butter side up). Close the lid and let the sandwich cook until golden brown.

PULLED TOFOO BARBECUE SLIDERS

This is finger-licking good, very messy and seriously easy to make. Perfect for summer parties and gatherings, just make sure you make enough of this dish for everyone to come back for seconds!

Serves: **4**
Preparation: **15 MINUTES**
Cooking: **25 MINUTES**

GET THIS STUFF

2 x 225g packs Smoked Tofoo, drained and dried
2 tbsp vegetable oil
2 tbsp dark soy sauce
1 tsp smoked paprika
1 tsp mild chilli powder
1 tsp garlic powder
200ml ready-made barbecue sauce
8 small bread rolls

For the apple slaw
½ red apple, cored and grated
½ green apple, cored and grated
½ red onion, very finely sliced
¼ white cabbage, finely shredded
3 tbsp mayonnaise
2 tbsp yoghurt, dairy or non-dairy
1 tsp wholegrain mustard
sea salt and ground black pepper

DO THIS STUFF

Preheat the oven to 180°C/160°C fan/350°F/gas mark 4. Line a baking tray with baking paper.

Grate the Tofoo on the big side of a grater and place in a mixing bowl. Add the vegetable oil, soy sauce, smoked paprika and the chilli and garlic powders, and toss until the Tofoo is well coated. Spoon the Tofoo on to the lined baking tray and bake for 20–25 minutes, tossing halfway through cooking.

Meanwhile, make the apple slaw. Mix together the apples, onion and cabbage. Mix together the mayonnaise, yoghurt and mustard, and fold into the apple, onion and cabbage. Toss to cover and season well.

Pour the barbecue sauce into a small saucepan and add a splash of water. Heat and leave to simmer.

Slice the bread rolls in half and lightly toast.

Add the Tofoo to the pan of simmering barbecue sauce and stir to coat. Spoon the 'pulled' Tofoo on to the toasted rolls and top with a spoonful of apple slaw. Serve immediately with a pile of napkins.

WHY NOT TRY:

· Topping with a spoonful of pineapple salsa.
· Dolloping with guacamole.

BANH MI

This fresh Vietnamese sandwich is stuffed with pickled vegetables, crunchy Tofoo, creamy mayonnaise, fresh coriander and a good kick of hot sauce. Make sure you keep any leftover pickled vegetables; they're delicious served on sandwiches or wraps. Use to top a burger, or serve alongside the Tofoo Katsu, a delicious accompaniment.

GET THIS STUFF

2 small baguettes (or one baguette, halved)
1 tbsp light soy sauce
zest of ½ lime, plus a squeeze of juice
1 tsp grated fresh ginger
1 garlic clove, minced
½ x 280g pack Naked Tofoo, drained, dried and thinly sliced
2 tbsp sunflower oil
2–4 tbsp mayonnaise
1 small bunch of coriander
freshly ground black pepper
a drizzle of sriracha

DO THIS STUFF

Mix together the soy sauce, lime zest, ginger and garlic in a shallow bowl. Add the Tofoo slices and marinate for 30 minutes.

Meanwhile, for the pickled vegetables, mix together the rice vinegar, sugar, spices and salt in a bowl. Add the carrot, cucumber, radishes and red chilli (if using) and lightly pickle for 10–20 minutes.

Halve the baguettes lengthways.

Heat a frying pan over a medium heat, add the oil and fry the Tofoo for 2–3 minutes on each side until it turns golden brown and crispy. Leave to cool.

Spread the baguette halves with the mayonnaise. Top with the pickled vegetables and the crispy Tofoo. Drizzle with sriracha and top with a handful of coriander. Season with black pepper and a squeeze of lime juice, and top with the other baguette half.

Serves: **2**
Preparation: **40 MINUTES**
Cooking: **5 MINUTES**

For the pickled vegetables
4 tbsp rice vinegar
4 tsp caster sugar
½ tsp fennel seeds
1 tsp coriander seeds
large pinch of sea salt
1 small carrot, peeled or
   scrubbed and cut into
   thin strips
¼ cucumber, cut into thin
   strips
2 radishes, sliced
1 red chilli, sliced and
   deseeded (optional)

WHY NOT TRY:

· Using this as a delicious filling for a jacket potato.
· Adding a jalapeño peppers to the baguette for an extra kick.

Image on the next page

BANH MI

TLT SANDWICH

These epic sandwiches are stuffed with Tofoo bacon, lettuce and tomatoes. They have three slices of bread so be ready to get a little messy while eating – it's worth it though, we promise.

Serves: **2**
Preparation: **1 HOUR+**
Cooking: **25 MINUTES**

GET THIS STUFF

1 x 225g pack Smoked Tofoo, drained, dried and cut into 5mm slices
1 small head of iceberg lettuce
3 large tomatoes, sliced
6 slices of wholemeal bread
3 tbsp mayonnaise

For the Tofoo bacon marinade
100ml light soy sauce
1 tbsp brown sauce
1 tbsp tomato ketchup
1 tsp white miso paste

DO THIS STUFF

Whisk together the Tofoo bacon marinade ingredients. Add the Tofoo slices and leave to marinate for a minimum of 1 hour.

Preheat the oven to 180°C/160°C fan/350°F/gas mark 4.

Line two baking trays with baking paper. Lay the marinated Tofoo slices on the trays and brush again with the marinade.

Bake the Tofoo for 10 minutes, then turn over and brush once again with the marinade. Return to the oven and bake for a further 5 minutes. The Tofoo bacon is ready when slightly crispy around the edges.

Spread one piece of bread with the mayonnaise and layer with some lettuce, sliced tomato and Tofoo bacon, then layer again with bread, mayonnaise, lettuce, tomato and Tofoo bacon, spread the final slice with mayo and squish on top of your TLT club. Hold together with a skewer, serve and enjoy.

WHY NOT TRY:

· Adding sliced avocado to your TLT.
· Stirring 1 teaspoon of wholegrain mustard into the mayonnaise.

HARISSA TOFOO STEAK GYRO

Harissa paste is an awesome ingredient to have to hand in your cupboard. As well as this fresh take on a Greek flatbread, you can add it to scrambled Tofoo, tomato pasta sauce or stews. Some pastes can be a little on the fiery side so do use sparingly.

Serves: **2**
Preparation: **5 MINUTES**
Cooking: **5 MINUTES**

GET THIS STUFF

1 tbsp sunflower oil
2 tbsp harissa paste
½ tsp fennel seeds
½ tsp smoked paprika
1 tbsp plain yoghurt, dairy or non-dairy
50g Naked Tofoo, drained, dried and cut into 4 slices
3 Little Gem lettuce leaves, shredded
2 flatbreads, warmed
½ red onion, sliced
1 cherry tomato, diced
1 tbsp tzatziki
squeeze of lemon juice
sea salt and freshly ground black pepper
a few mint leaves

DO THIS STUFF

Mix together the oil, harissa paste, fennel seeds, smoked paprika and yoghurt. Add the Tofoo and toss until coated. Leave for as long as you can so the flavours can develop.

Heat a griddle pan until hot, reduce the heat to medium and add the Tofoo slices. Griddle for about 2 minutes on each side or until the Tofoo is hot and comes away easily from the pan.

To assemble, place the lettuce leaves on the flatbread and top with the Tofoo. Sprinkle with the red onion, tomato and a spoonful of tzatziki.

Squeeze over some lemon juice and season with salt and black pepper. Garnish with the mint. Roll and eat immediately.

WHY NOT TRY:

· Spreading the flatbread with hummus for added creaminess.
· Adding avocado for freshness and cucumber cubes for crunch.

TOFOO FAJITAS

Saturday night should always be fajita night. Serve with bowls of salsa, guacamole and yoghurt, and let everyone craft their own fajitas for some foodie fun.

Serves: **4**
Preparation: **10 MINUTES**
Cooking: **10 MINUTES**

GET THIS STUFF

1 x 225g pack Smoked Tofoo, drained, dried and cut into 16 strips
2 tbsp cornflour
2 tsp smoked paprika
3 tbsp sunflower oil
1 red pepper, deseeded and cut into strips
1 green pepper, deseeded and cut into strips
1 yellow pepper, deseeded and cut into strips
1 red onion, sliced
½ tsp ground cumin
½ tsp ground coriander
½ tsp garlic powder
sea salt and freshly ground black pepper

To serve
8 tortillas
yoghurt
guacamole, homemade or shop-bought
handful of coriander, roughly chopped
lime wedges

DO THIS STUFF

Dry the Tofoo strips with kitchen paper. Sprinkle the cornflour and paprika over a plate and roll the Tofoo strips in the spiced cornflour.

Heat 2 tablespoons of oil in a frying pan over a medium heat until hot. Add the Tofoo strips and fry for 3–4 minutes, turning once or twice, until golden brown and crisp. Drain on a plate lined with kitchen paper.

Reduce the heat and add more oil, if necessary. Add the peppers and onion to the pan and stir-fry for 3 minutes. Stir in the spices and 2 tablespoons of water, and cook for a further 2–3 minutes. Season with a little salt and lots of black pepper.

Warm the tortillas following the pack instructions.

To serve, pile some vegetables on to the warmed tortillas and top with the Tofoo. Top with some yoghurt, guacamole, coriander and a squeeze of lime juice. Wrap up and serve.

See page 190 for how to make your own guac!

WHY NOT TRY:

· Adding a fresh tomato salsa for a burst of freshness.
· Adding sliced courgette or butternut squash to the mix.

BANG BANG TOFOO BAGELS

You can keep this bang bang sauce on the milder side if you want a little less 'bang' or go punchy by adding a good pinch of chilli flakes. The choice is yours, and it's delicious either way.

Serves: **4**
Preparation: **15 MINUTES**
Cooking: **10 MINUTES**

GET THIS STUFF

1 tbsp cornflour
1 x 225g pack Smoked Tofoo, drained, dried and cut into 8 slices
1 tbsp sunflower oil
4 bagels, halved
1 carrot, peeled or scrubbed, cut into thin ribbons
2 spring onions, cut on the diagonal
1 tsp black sesame seeds
pinch of chilli flakes (optional)
juice of 1 lime

For the bang bang sauce
50g smooth peanut butter
2 tbsp sweet chilli sauce
1 tsp toasted sesame oil
1 tbsp dark soy sauce
pinch of chilli flakes (optional)

DO THIS STUFF

For the bang bang sauce, mix together the peanut butter, sweet chilli sauce, sesame oil and soy sauce. Taste and adjust the seasoning with a pinch of chilli flakes or some extra soy sauce. If the sauce is a little thick, loosen with some water.

Place the cornflour in a shallow bowl. Dry each slice of Tofoo with kitchen paper and dip in the cornflour, covering completely.

Heat the oil in a large frying pan over a medium heat and fry the Tofoo for 5 minutes, turn over, and cook for a further 5 minutues or until lightly golden and crisp.

Lightly toast the bagels and top with a bed of carrot ribbons. Top with Tofoo slices. Spoon over the sauce. Sprinkle with the spring onions, black sesame seeds and chilli flakes (if using). Squeeze over the lime juice. Top with the other bagel halves.

WHY NOT TRY:

· Using this bang bang sauce as a salad dressing. Loosen with water until you get a drizzling consistency.
· Leaving out the bagel and serving with a handful of salad leaves instead.

PANKO TOFOO BAO BUNS
with pickled onions

These fluffy, light bao buns are sure to impress, especially when stuffed with crispy panko Tofoo. You can grab ready-made bao buns in most supermarkets nowadays. Easy-peasy.

GET THIS STUFF

250g Naked Tofoo, drained, dried and cut into 8 strips
75g cornflour
1 tbsp Chinese 5 spice
2 tbsp light soy sauce
75g panko breadcrumbs
2 tbsp sesame seeds
sunflower oil, for frying

For the pickled red onion
1 large red onion, sliced thinly into rings
150ml apple cider vinegar
2 tbsp granulated sugar
1 tsp sea salt and freshly ground black pepper
1 star anise
4 coriander seeds

DO THIS STUFF

For the pickled onion, place the onion into a sieve or colander. Boil the kettle and pour the boiling water over the onion. Leave until cool enough to handle.

In the container or jar you will be using to store the onion pickle, add the vinegar, sugar, salt, pepper and spices. Stir to dissolve. Add the onions and gently stir. The onions will be ready in about 30 minutes, but are better after a few hours. Store in the refrigerator.

Dry each strip of Tofoo with kitchen paper.

Line up three flat plates. Mix together the cornflour and Chinese 5 spice and place on the first plate. Pour the soy sauce on to plate number two. Mix together the panko breadcrumbs and sesame seeds and place on the third plate.

Take one Tofoo strip at a time and dust completely in the cornflour, knock off any loose cornflour and dust again. Dip in the soy sauce until completely saturated. Finally, dip in the panko breadcrumb and sesame mixture. Press the Tofoo strips down a little to make the coating stick. Coat all sides.

To serve

8 shop-bought bao buns

¼ cucumber, sliced

50g beansprouts

handful of coriander, ripped

Heat 1cm of oil in a large frying pan and cook the Tofoo strips for about 2–3 minutes on each side. Cook until all sides are golden brown and crunchy. Do not overcrowd the frying pan and cook the Tofoo in two batches if necessary.

Heat the bao buns following the pack instructions. Fill the buns with the fried Tofoo, cucumber, beansprouts and top with pickled onions and coriander. Serve immediately.

* Any leftover pickled onions can be kept and stored in the fridge. They will keep for several weeks, but are at their best in the first week

Image on the next page

WHY NOT TRY:

· Replacing the pickled onions with kimchi.

· Serving these crunchy Tofoo fingers in wraps or baps or even in a salad.

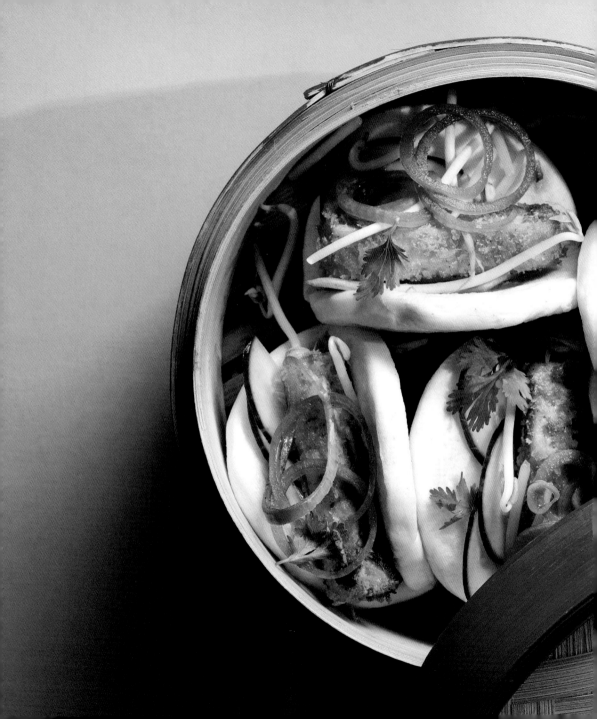

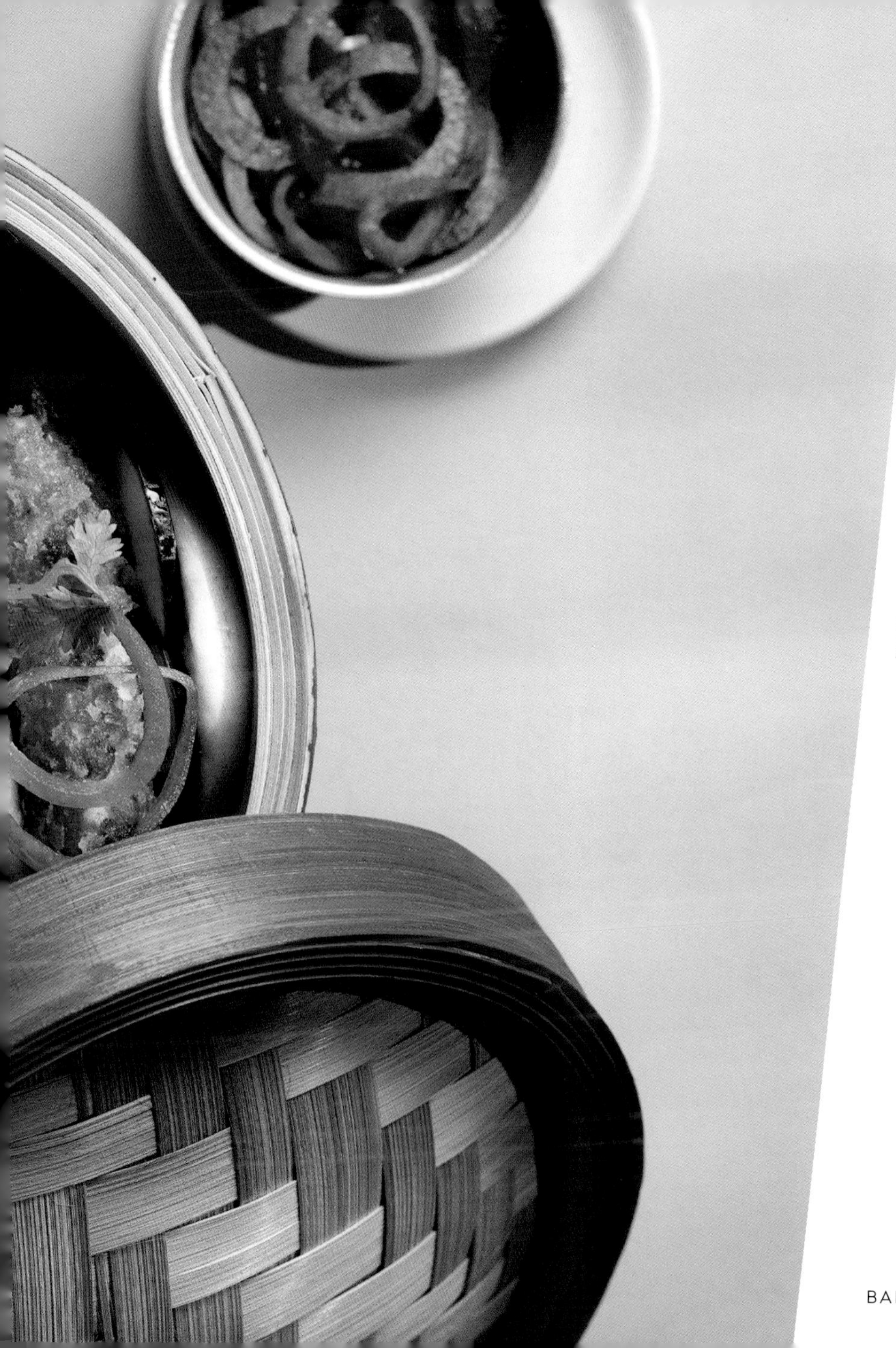

PANKO TOFOO BAO BUNS WITH PICKLED ONIONS

SMOKED TOFOO 'TIKTOK' QUESADILLAS

A social media star – these quesadillas are just a funky, folded version of quesadillas that make them even easier to hungrily put away or wrap up for lunch on the move.

Serves: **2**
Preparation: **10 MINUTES**
Cooking: **5 MINUTES**

GET THIS STUFF

1 avocado
1 tsp sriracha or hot sauce
2 large flour tortillas
1 x 225g pack Smoked Tofoo, drained, dried and crumbled
1 roasted red pepper from a jar, drained and sliced
4 spring onions, thinly sliced
100g cheese, such as Cheddar, mozzarella or vegan, grated
2 tsp olive oil

DO THIS STUFF

Remove the stone from the avocado and spoon the flesh into a bowl. Add the sriracha or hot sauce to your liking. Mash together.

Place one wrap on a chopping board. Using a knife, make a slit from the centre to the edge at the bottom of the wrap, directly in front of you (six o'clock). Now imagine dividing the wrap into four quarters.

Starting by the cut, going clockwise, add a quarter of the avocado to one quarter and spread evenly. Spoon half the Tofoo on to the following quarter. Next, pile on half the red pepper and spring onion on the third quarter. Pile half the cheese on to the final quarter.

Starting with the avocado, fold up and work your way around clockwise. Now, you're going to be left with a perfectly folded triangular wrap. Repeat with the other wrap and remaining filling ingredients.

Heat the oil in a large frying pan over a medium heat, add one or both wraps and cook for 1–2 minutes on each side until they are browned and crispy on both sides. Serve immediately.

WHY NOT TRY:

· Adding refried beans, salsa, tomatoes or sweetcorn.
· Tossing the Tofoo in Cajun seasoning for added spice.
· Sprinkling with finely chopped red chilli for added heat.

SMOKED TOFOO, PICKLED CABBAGE & RICE BURRITOS

Using microwavable rice makes these burritos so easy, a little cheat that goes a long way – don't worry, we won't tell anyone! Try flavoured rice such as chilli and lime or roasted vegetables for a little added somethin' somethin'.

GET THIS STUFF

For the burrito
1 tbsp sunflower oil
1 small onion, chopped
1 tsp ground cumin
1 tsp ground turmeric
1 x 225g pack Smoked Tofoo, drained, dried and cut into 1.5cm cubes
2 tbsp sliced jalapeños from a jar, drained
1 x 250g pack microwave basmati rice
4 large tortillas wraps
½ iceberg lettuce, shredded
1 avocado, mashed
6 tbsp mozzarella, grated
4 tbsp soured cream or yoghurt

DO THIS STUFF

For the pickled cabbage, place the cabbage in a colander, set over a heatproof bowl or above the sink. Pour over 1 litre of boiling water. Drain well. Transfer the cabbage to a large jar, add the spring onions and red chilli, and mix.

Combine the vinegar and sugar in a saucepan over a high heat and bring to the boil. Remove from the heat and leave to cool slightly, then pour over cabbage, stirring to combine. Leave to pickle for 30 minutes before using, but the longer you leave the cabbage the more the flavour develops, and the harshness of the vinegar mellows.

Heat the oil in a large frying pan over medium-high heat. Add the onion and cook for about 5 minutes or until starting to turn golden. Add the cumin and turmeric, and stir for 30 seconds. Add the Tofoo and jalapeños, and cook for about 3 minutes. Remove from the heat.

For the pickled cabbage
½ red cabbage, shredded
6 spring onions, sliced
1 red chilli, deseeded and
   finely chopped
150ml apple cider vinegar
1 tbsp granulated sugar

Meanwhile, cook the rice following the pack instructions.

Warm the tortillas in a dry frying pan or in the microwave. Layer each tortilla with lettuce, Tofoo mix, rice and avocado, then top with cheese and the pickled cabbage. Finally, drizzle with the soured cream or yoghurt. Wrap and roll the tortillas, cut in half and serve.

WHY NOT TRY:

· Using kimchi or coleslaw instead of the pickled cabbage.
· Smothering the tortillas with hummus for an added layer of flavour.

TOFISH FINGER SANDWICH

A fresh take on a classic, and the perfect lunch.
Ideally enjoyed by the sea on a slightly chilly day.

Serves: **4**
Preparation: **5 MINUTES**
Marinating: **30 MINUTES**
Cooking: **15-20 MINUTES**

GET THIS STUFF

For the Tofish fingers
1 tbsp dark soy sauce
juice of ½ lemon
2 x 280g packs Naked
   Tofoo, drained, dried
   and cut into 6 strips
4 tbsp cornflour
50g panko or fresh
   readcrumbs
vegetable oil, for
   deep-frying
salt

To serve
4 crusty rolls
tomato ketchup or
   mayonnaise
4 gherkins, sliced
   lengthways

DO THIS STUFF

Mix together the soy sauce, lemon juice and a pinch of salt. Add the Tofoo slices and leave to marinate for 30 minutes.

When ready to cook, tip the cornflour into a shallow bowl. In another shallow bowl, mix the breadcrumbs with a generous pinch of salt.

Remove the Tofoo from the marinade and dip in the cornflour to coat. Dip again in the marinade and then coat in the breadcrumbs, pressing and turning until evenly coated.

Heat 2–3cm of oil in a deep frying pan over a medium heat. Drop a piece of Tofoo into the oil, if it sizzles it is ready to start cooking. Carefully lower the Tofoo fingers in and fry for 2 minutes on each side until golden and crisp. You'll need to do this in batches as crowding the oil will stop the crumbs getting crunchy. Remove and transfer to a plate lined with kitchen paper to drain.

Split the rolls open and spread with the ketchup or mayonnaise. Add three Tofish fingers to each roll and top with the sliced gherkins.

WHY NOT TRY:

· Adding Little Gem lettuce for crunch.
· Serving the Tofish fingers in a wrap.

Enjoy and remember plenty of napkins!

TOFOO & CARROT FALAFEL FLATBREADS

Don't let the number of ingredients in this recipe put you off, it's super easy and super, super tasty. Give these flatbreads a go; we just know they'll become a staple in your recipe repertoire.

GET THIS STUFF

For the falafels
100g carrots, peeled or scrubbed, finely grated
½ tsp ground cumin
½ tsp ground coriander
1 x 400g can chickpeas, drained and rinsed
1 red chilli, deseeded and diced
1 garlic clove, crushed
zest of 1 lemon
a bunch of coriander, finely chopped, plus extra to serve
1 tbsp plain flour
½ tsp baking powder
½ x 280g pack Naked Tofoo, drained, dried and crumbled
sunflower oil, for shallow-frying
sea salt and freshly ground black pepper

DO THIS STUFF

Place the carrots on kitchen paper and squeeze the moisture out of them and pat dry. Transfer to a food processor and add the ground spices, chickpeas, chilli, garlic, lemon zest, coriander, flour, baking powder and some seasoning. Whizz until combined. Add the Tofoo and pulse, just to combine the mixture – do not over-blend.

Divide the mixture into 12 equal-sized portions and shape each one into a small ball. Flatten the balls slightly with your hands. Cover and chill in the fridge for at least 30 minutes to firm them up.

Meanwhile, make the flatbreads. In a large bowl, mix the flour, baking powder and salt. Stir in the yoghurt, then mix with your hands until the dough comes together.

Knead the dough for 5 minutes until it is smooth and elastic. If the dough is sticky, add a little more flour. Wrap the dough in clingfilm and leave it to rest in the fridge for 10–15 minutes.

Heat a frying pan over a medium heat and brush a thin layer of sunflower oil onto the base of the pan.

Serves: **4**

Preparation: **30 MINUTES**

Cooking: **25 MINUTES+**
(depending on the size of
your pans)

For the flatbreads
400g self-raising flour
1 tsp baking powder
pinch of salt
350g coconut or
   Greek yoghurt

To serve
hummus, homemade
   (see page 62) or
   shop-bought

Divide the dough into eight pieces and roll or flatten into thin oval shapes. Cook the flatbreads, one or two at a time, depending on size of your pan, for 2 minutes until the bread inflates and the lower side is golden. Flip and cook for a further 1 minute until golden and cooked on both sides. Repeat with the remaining dough, keeping the flatbreads warm in a clean tea towel.

Heat 1cm of oil in a large frying pan over a medium heat and, when it's hot, add the falafels in batches so you don't overcrowd the pan. Cook the falafels for about 2 minutes on each side or until crisp and golden brown. Remove from the pan and drain on kitchen paper.

Serve the falafels alongside the flatbreads and hummus with a generous scattering of coriander.

Image on the
next page

WHY NOT TRY:

- Swapping out the carrots for beetroot or butternut squash.
- Serving pickled cabbage (see page 55) or onion with these falafels for added tartness.

TOFOO & CARROT FALAFEL FLATBREADS

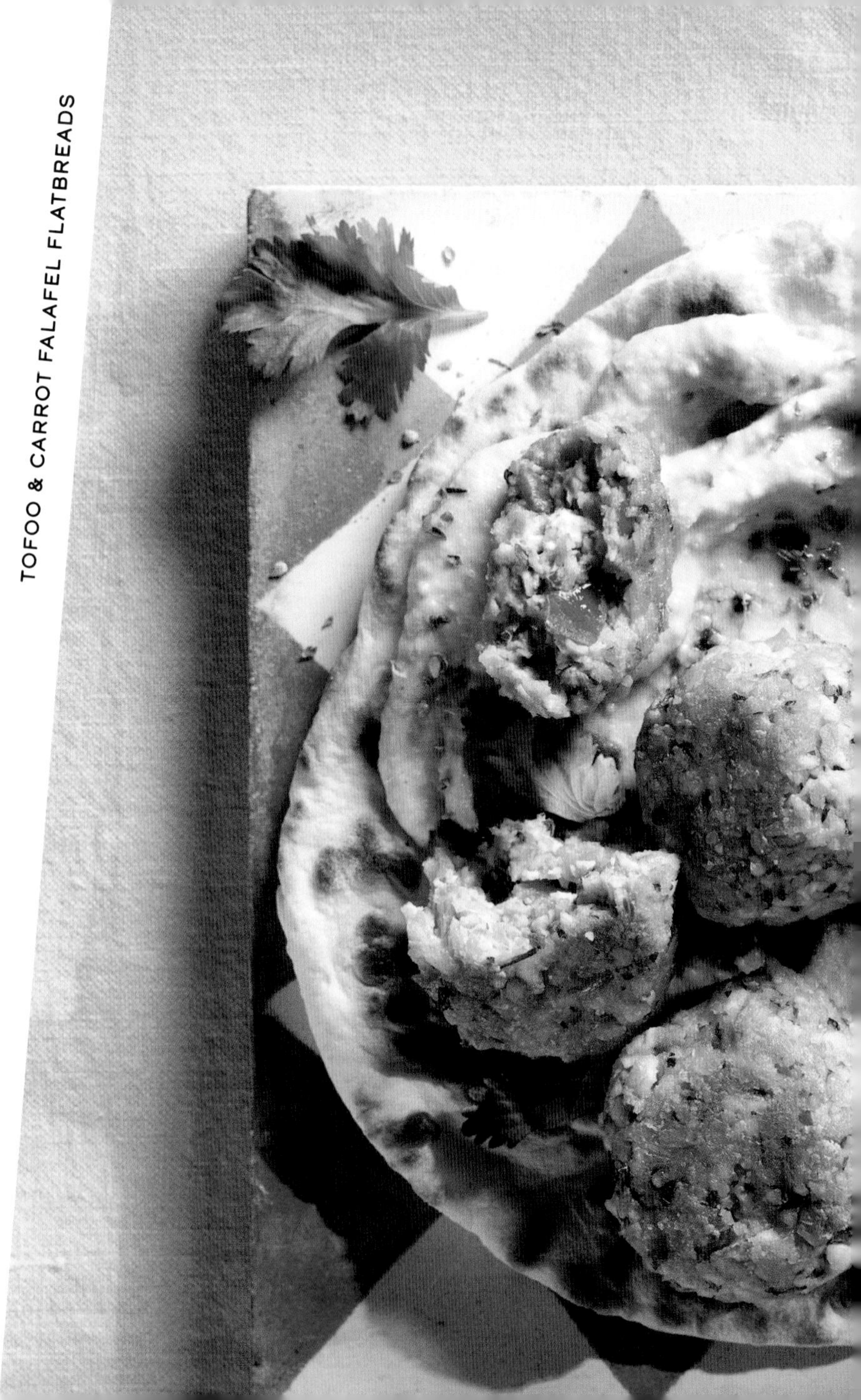

TOFOO BAGEL
with red pepper hummus

Simple but delicious. The perfect lunch. We said it. *Perfect.*

Serves: **4**
Preparation: **10 MINUTES**
Cooking: **5 MINUTES**

GET THIS STUFF

1 x 280g pack Naked
    Tofoo, drained, dried
    and cut into 4 slices
1 tbsp cornflour
2 tbsp sumac
1 tbsp sunflower oil
4 seeded bagels, halved
1 carrot, peeled or
    scrubbed, grated
50g rocket

For the hummus
1 x 400g can chickpeas,
    drained and rinsed
juice of 1 lemon
2 garlic cloves, crushed
1 roasted red pepper from
    a jar, drained
2 tbsp tahini
1 tbsp olive oil
sea salt

DO THIS STUFF

For the hummus, tip the chickpeas into a food processor. Add the lemon juice, garlic, red pepper, tahini and oil, and whizz together. Season with a pinch of sea salt, then use a spatula to scrape the hummus down the sides of the bowl and whizz again until smooth.

Dry each slice of Tofoo with kitchen paper. Mix together the cornflour and sumac, add the Tofoo and coat well.

Heat the oil in a pan and get it as hot as you can. Reduce the heat to medium and fry the Tofoo for about 5 minutes, turning throughout, until it's golden brown.

Lightly toast the bagels. Layer the hummus, Tofoo, grated carrot and rocket on the bottom half of the bagels. Top with the other halves. Serve immediately.

See? Perfect

WHY NOT TRY:

- Using ready-made flavoured hummus such as beetroot, chilli or roasted pepper for an even quicker lunch.
- Pea shoots or watercress would also be delicious in these bagels.

TOFOO VIETNAMESE SPRING ROLLS

These spring rolls are super fresh and crunchy. Perfect for lunch, or a starter ... or a snack.

Serves: **4**
Preparation: **20 MINUTES**
Cooking: **20 MINUTES**

GET THIS STUFF

- ½ x 280g pack Naked Tofoo, drained, dried and cut into 5mm slices
- 2 tbsp dark soy sauce
- 1 tbsp hot chilli or sweet chilli sauce, plus extra for dipping
- 1 tbsp coconut oil
- 12 rice paper wrappers or rice paper spring roll wrappers
- handful of mint leaves
- 1 Little Gem lettuce, leaves separated
- 1 red pepper, deseeded and cut into matchsticks
- 1 carrot, peeled and cut into matchsticks
- 75g beansprouts
- 1 cucumber, cut into thin strips

DO THIS STUFF

Preheat the oven to 180°C/160°C fan/350°F/gas mark 4.

Place the Tofoo in a shallow bowl. Mix together the soy sauce, chilli sauce and coconut oil. Pour over the Tofoo and gently mix to cover.

Spread the Tofoo evenly over a baking sheet and cook for 10 minutes. Turn the Tofoo slices over and brush with any remaining marinade. Bake for a further 10 minutes. Once the Tofoo is crispy on the outside, remove from the oven and slice into strips.

When ready to make the rolls, prepare and line up all the ingredients.

Fill a large bowl with warm water. Working one roll at a time. Quickly dip each rice paper wrapper in warm water for a few seconds and lay on a chopping board and leave for 30 seconds.

Lay some mint, lettuce, vegetables and Tofoo strips down the middle of the wrap.

Roll the wrapper over the fillings, tucking and rolling the wrapper with your fingers, making sure all the fillings remain tight and round within the rice paper wrapper. Continue rolling to seal the seam. Repeat with the remaining filling and wrappers. Serve alongside some chilli sauce.

WHY NOT TRY:

- Filling with vermicelli noodles, avocado or rocket along with the Tofoo.
- A peanut sauce instead of the chilli sauce.

HOISIN TOFOO PANCAKES

This fakeaway will soon become a firm Saturday night favourite. Serve with a cold beer and plenty of napkins. It's going to get messy.

Serves: **4**
Preparation: **15 MINUTES**
Cooking: **15 MINUTES**

GET THIS STUFF

1 x 280g pack Naked Tofoo, drained, dried and cut into 16 strips
2 tbsp cornflour
2 tbsp Chinese 5 spice
1 tsp garlic powder
1–2 tbsp vegetable oil
8 Chinese pancakes
6–8 tbsp hoisin sauce
½ cucumber, cut into matchsticks
4 spring onions, shredded lengthways
freshly ground black pepper

DO THIS STUFF

Dry each strip of Tofoo really well with kitchen paper. Mix together the cornflour, Chinese 5 spice and garlic powder. Sprinkle over the Tofoo strips and coat them thoroughly in the mixture.

Heat 1 tablespoon of oil in a large frying pan and add the Tofoo, making sure not to overcrowd the pan. You may need to do this in batches. Cook the Tofoo, turning the strips over, for about 7 minutes or until the Tofoo is golden brown and crunchy. Remove from the pan and season with black pepper.

Once the Tofoo is cooked, warm the pancakes in the microwave by following the pack instructions.

To serve, spread each pancake with a little hoisin sauce. Top with the cucumber, spring onions and a pile of Tofoo strips. Roll and enjoy.

WHY NOT TRY:

· Serving with blanched pak choi, beansprouts or shredded carrots.
· You can also chuck these Tofoo strips in a salad or stir-fry.

SESAME TOFOO TOAST

The perfect starter to any homemade Chinese meal. We challenge you to stop after just one ...

Serves: **4**
Preparation: **20 MINUTES**
Cooking: **20 MINUTES**

GET THIS STUFF

1 x 280g pack Naked Tofoo, drained, dried and cut into 1cm cubes
2cm piece of fresh ginger, peeled and chopped
1 garlic clove, finely chopped
2 spring onions, sliced
1 tsp cornflour
½ tsp light soy sauce, plus extra to serve
½ tsp toasted sesame oil
4 slices of white bread
3 tbsp sesame seeds
sunflower oil, for frying
sweet chilli sauce, to serve

DO THIS STUFF

Dry the Tofoo really well with kitchen paper. Place the Tofoo, ginger, garlic, spring onions, cornflour, soy sauce and sesame oil in a food processor and whizz to a thick paste.

Cut each slice of bread into four triangles. Spread the filling on each bread triangle. Roll and press the sesame seeds on to the filling side of the bread.

Heat 2cm of oil in a deep frying pan, making sure it is hot enough to toast a square of bread in a few seconds.

Add the first triangle, Tofoo side up, and fry for 2 minutes until you have a crispy golden base. Carefully flip over and cook for a further 2 minutes on the other side until crisp.

Drain the cooked toast on kitchen paper while you fry the remaining triangles.

Serve the Tofoo toast alongside the sweet chilli and soy sauces.

WHY NOT TRY:

Making a double batch and freezing. These bad boys keep for three months and only take about 10 minutes in the oven to reheat through completely, while keeping their crisp texture.

SHAWARMA-SPICED TOFOO PITTA WRAPS

Shawarma is one of the most popular street foods in the world. Traditionally it is a Levantine Arab dish made of meat cut into thin slices, stacked in a cone-like shape, and spit-roasted. This recipe takes the essence of this famous street food but roasts it in an oven for a more home-friendly version.

Serves: **4**
Preparation: **10 MINUTES**
Cooking: **25 MINUTES**

GET THIS STUFF

½ small red onion, thinly sliced
3 tbsp rice wine vinegar
1 x 280g pack Naked Tofoo, drained and dried
3 tbsp olive oil
2 tsp ground coriander
2 tsp sweet paprika
½ tsp ground cinnamon
1 tbsp lemon juice
1 small garlic clove, finely grated
2 tbsp fresh mint, chopped, plus extra to serve
150g Greek yoghurt
4 pittas, warmed
2 mini cucumbers, thinly sliced lengthways
4 baby plum tomatoes, halved
sea salt

DO THIS STUFF

Preheat the oven to 180°C/160°C fan/350°F/gas mark 4.

Mix together the onion and vinegar in a small bowl to coat and set aside.

Tear the Tofoo into ragged pieces and arrange in a single layer on a baking tray. Mix together the oil, ground coriander, paprika, cinnamon, lemon juice and 1 teaspoon of salt. Pour over the Tofoo and toss well to coat.

Roast the Tofoo for 20–25 minutes, turning once or twice, until crispy around the edges and well browned.

Stir the garlic and mint into the yoghurt and season with salt.

Serve by spooning a dollop of yoghurt on to the pittas followed by some crisp Tofoo, cucumber, tomato, drained pickled onions and a scattering of mint. Roll or fold the pitta and enjoy.

WHY NOT TRY:

Serving this with a herby couscous.

3
Soups & Salads

ROAST TOMATO SOUP
with pesto Tofoo croutons

These Tofoo croutons are a brilliant way to add protein to a soup. For packed lunches, store the soup and croutons separately and add the Tofoo once the soup is heated to avoid the croutons becoming mushy.

Serves: **4**

Preparation: **20 MINUTES**

Cooking: **1 HOUR 15 MINUTES**

GET THIS STUFF

1kg large, ripe tomatoes (a selection of tomatoes would be nice but is not essential)

1 red pepper, deseeded and cut into chunks

2 celery sticks, cut into large chunks

1 onion, cut into wedges

4 large garlic cloves, crushed

1 tsp dried oregano

2–3 tbsp olive oil

1 litre vegetable stock

handful of basil leaves

sea salt freshly ground black pepper

For the Tofoo croutons

½ x 225g pack Smoked Tofoo, drained, dried and ripped into bite-sized pieces

1–2 tbsp basil pesto

2 tsp olive oil

DO THIS STUFF

Preheat the oven to 200°C/180°C fan/400°F/gas mark 6.

Halve the tomatoes and place, cut-side up, in a large roasting tin. Fit the red pepper, celery and onion around the tomatoes, scatter over the garlic, sprinkle with the oregano and season with black pepper. Drizzle with the olive oil and toss gently. Roast for 50 minutes–1 hour, or until the vegetables are soft.

Remove the roasting tin from the oven and add the stock, scraping all the goodness from the bottom of the pan. Blitz with a hand blender or in a food processor until smooth. Very carefully pour back into a large saucepan and heat gently. Check the seasoning, adding salt and black pepper as needed.

To make the croutons, toss together the Tofoo, pesto and half the oil. Heat the remaining oil in a pan and cook the Tofoo for 3–4 minutes until lightly crisp.

Serve the soup topped with the Tofoo croutons and basil leaves.

WHY NOT TRY:

- Serving these delicious pesto Tofoo croutons in a salad.
- Making your own pesto, such as the kale version on page 189.

MISO & TOFOO SOUP

Miso soup is a classic comfort dish and the perfect quick, healthy lunchtime soup.

Serves: **2**
Preparation: **5 MINUTES**
Cooking: **10 MINUTES**

GET THIS STUFF

- 1 litre good-quality vegetable stock
- 3–4 tbsp white or yellow miso paste
- 50g spring greens, chopped
- ½ x 280g pack Naked Tofoo, drained, dried and diced
- 1 tsp shredded nori seaweed
- 4 spring onions, sliced

DO THIS STUFF

Pour the stock into a pan and bring to a simmer. Spoon the miso paste into a small bowl and add 1 tablespoon of hot water and mix until smooth. Add to the stock and whisk to combine.

Add the spring greens and Tofoo to the stock and cook for 5 minutes.

Spoon into two bowls and serve sprinkled with the shredded nori and spring onions.

The perfect cosy lunch!

WHY NOT TRY:

Adding frozen peas or spinach.

SEARED SESAME TOFOO STEAKS
with noodle salad

Looking for some extra greens in your salad? Make use of seasonal vegetables such as asparagus, peas or broad beans for added freshness in this dish.

Serves: **2**
Preparation: **10 MINUTES**
Cooking: **10 MINUTES**

GET THIS STUFF

1 x 280g pack Naked Tofoo, drained, dried and sliced in half
1–2 tbsp sesame seeds
2 tbsp sunflower oil
coriander leaves, to serve

For the noodle salad
1 red chilli, deseeded and chopped
2 tbsp dark soy sauce
2 tbsp caster sugar
2 tbsp rice wine vinegar
200g egg noodles
10 sugar snap peas, halved
5 baby corns, halved
1 carrot, peeled and grated
4 spring onions, finely sliced

DO THIS STUFF

Sprinkle the Tofoo steaks with the sesame seeds.

Place the chilli, soy sauce, caster sugar and rice wine vinegar in a small jar or bowl and shake or whisk until the dressing is combined.

Cook the noodles following the pack instructions and drain. Add the sugar snap peas, baby corn, carrots and spring onions to the warm noodles, drizzle with half the dressing and toss together.

Heat a frying pan with the sunflower oil until very hot, then reduce the heat to medium, add the Tofoo and cook for about 3–4 minutes on each side until golden brown and crisp.

Make sure you cook the edges of the Tofoo steaks as well as both sides

Divide the noodles between two plates, top with the Tofoo steaks, drizzle with the remaining dressing and scatter with coriander to serve.

WHY NOT TRY:

· Griddling the Tofoo steak for added smokiness.
· Making double the quantity of the dressing and storing in a glass jar in the fridge for up to two weeks so it's ready to use.

TOFOO POKE BOWL

Poke (pronounced poh-key) means to cut or slice in Hawaiian. It refers to various colourful toppings arranged and served over rice.

Serves: **2**
Preparation: **20 MINUTES**
Marinating: **30+ MINUTES**

GET THIS STUFF

1 x 280g pack Naked
   Tofoo, drained, dried
   and cut into 2cm cubes
200g cooked wholegrain
   rice or cooked quinoa
½ cucumber, thinly sliced
4 radishes, sliced
¼ red cabbage, shredded
1 carrot, peeled and cut
   into thin ribbons
1 avocado, thinly sliced
1 tbsp black or white
   sesame seeds

For the Tofoo marinade
4 tbsp light soy sauce
1 tbsp rice wine vinegar
½ tbsp sambal oelek
   (optional)
1 tsp sesame oil
1 garlic clove, crushed
2cm piece of fresh ginger,
   peeled and finely chopped

To serve
handful of coriander leaves
lime wedges

DO THIS STUFF

Mix together the Tofoo marinade ingredients in a shallow dish. Add the Tofoo, toss until completely covered and leave to marinate for at least 30 minutes. When ready to serve, drain the Tofoo, reserving the excess marinade.

Divide the rice or quinoa between two shallow bowls. Top with the drained Tofoo, cucumber, radishes and cabbage. Roll the carrots into roses, fan the avocado and add to the bowl. Drizzle with the reserved marinade. Just before serving, sprinkle with the sesame seeds and coriander and serve with lime wedges.

*Do your best rainbow interpretation when choosing your combination of vegetables – the more colour, the better

WHY NOT TRY:

· Frying the marinated Tofoo for added crunch.
· Adding cubes of mango for extra freshness.

TOFETA GREEK SALAD

This Greek salad has everything you'd expect! Cucumbers, peppers, tomatoes, olives, onion, oh ... and chunks of sharp Tofeta, of course. Serve with a glass of crisp white wine and eat in the sunshine for ultimate summer vibes.

Serves: **4**
Preparation: **20 MINUTES**
Marinating: **AS LONG AS POSSIBLE**

GET THIS STUFF

For the Tofeta
1 tbsp sea salt
½ tbsp garlic powder
½ tbsp caster sugar
½ tbsp dried oregano
½ tsp freshly ground
   black pepper
175ml olive oil
80ml white wine vinegar
1 x 280g pack Naked
   Tofoo, drained, dried
   and cut into small cubes
3 tbsp nutritional yeast
   flakes

For the Greek Salad
1 cucumber, quartered and
   chopped
4 large ripe tomatoes,
   quartered
1 green pepper, deseeded
   and chopped
1 red onion, sliced
handful of Kalamata olives,
   pitted

DO THIS STUFF

For the Tofeta, mix together the sea salt, garlic powder, sugar, oregano and black pepper in a jar with a lid or by using a medium-sized bowl. Add the oil, vinegar and 3 tablespoons of water. Shake or whisk well.

In a medium-sized bowl, gently mix the Tofoo with the nutritional yeast. Shake the salad dressing and pour half over the Tofoo. Cover and marinate for as long as you can, or overnight in the fridge, if possible.

When ready to serve the salad, transfer the prepared vegetables to a large bowl.

Add the Tofoo and its marinade to the salad. Pour over the reserved marinade and toss gently. Serve with fresh crusty bread.

WHY NOT TRY:

· If there is any Tofeta left over, store it in the fridge. It's great thrown on a pizza, tossed in a salad or added to a wrap.
· Adding a pinch of chilli flakes for an extra kick.

CRISPY TOFOO RAMEN

Super fresh, super easy and super delicious.
Get slurping!

For the crispy Tofoo
2 tbsp light soy sauce
1 tsp toasted sesame oil
1 tsp maple syrup
1 x 280g pack Naked
    Tofoo, drained, dried
    and cut in half, then into
    4 thick slices
1 tbsp cornflour
2 tbsp sunflower oil

For the stock
700ml vegetable stock
2 tbsp light soy sauce, plus
    extra to taste (optional)
1 tbsp miso paste
3 garlic cloves, sliced
2cm piece of fresh ginger,
    peeled and sliced
pinch of chilli flakes
1 tsp Chinese 5 spice
½ tsp caster sugar, plus
    extra to taste (optional)
375g ramen noodles

For the crispy Tofoo, mix together the soy sauce, sesame oil and maple syrup in a bowl. Add the Tofoo and leave to marinate for at least 15 minutes, but longer will enhance the flavour.

For the broth, mix together the stock, soy sauce, miso paste, garlic, ginger, chili flakes, Chinese 5 spice, sugar and 300ml water in a large saucepan. Bring the mixture to the boil, reduce the heat and simmer for 5 minutes. Taste the stock and adjust the taste to your liking with more soy sauce or sugar. Keep warm while preparing the other ingredients.

When ready to serve the ramen, sprinkle the cornflour over a flat plate. Remove the Tofoo from the marinade. Dip the Tofoo in the cornflour until completely covered.

Heat the oil in a shallow frying pan. When hot, add the Tofoo and cook for about 2 minutes on each side until it is golden brown and crispy.

Cook the ramen noodles following the pack instructions. Drain.

Serves: **4**
Preparation: **15 MINUTES**
Marinating: **15+ MINUTES**
Cooking: **15 MINUTES**

To serve
4 tbsp sweetcorn
2 baby pak choi, leaves
  separated
4 spring onions, sliced
1 sheet of nori seaweed,
  shredded
handful of micro herbs

Divide the noodles between four bowls and top with the sweetcorn, pak choi and spring onions.

Strain the stock using a sieve, then return to the pan and bring back to the boil once more. Divide the stock between the four bowls. Add the Tofoo and sprinkle with the shredded nori and micro herbs to serve.

Image on the next page

WHY NOT TRY:

· Adding cooked mushrooms to the broth.
· Experimenting with different noodles such as soba, udon or rice noodles.
· If you're not vegan, serve topped with a boiled egg.

TOFOO PANZANELLA SALAD

Panzanella is originally a Tuscan salad of soaked stale bread, onions and tomatoes that is popular in the summer. This is even more delicious if made a day ahead so there's time for all the flavours to combine.

Serves: **4**

Preparation: **45+ MINUTES**

Cooking: **25 MINUTES**

GET THIS STUFF

1kg mixed ripe tomatoes, cut into bite-sized pieces*

1 stale ciabatta or country loaf, ripped into chunks

1 x 225g pack Smoked Tofoo, drained, dried and ripped into chunks

130ml extra virgin olive oil

1 shallot, finely chopped

2 garlic cloves, crushed

½ tsp Dijon mustard

1 tbsp white wine vinegar

handful of basil leaves, ripped

sea salt and freshly ground black pepper

* Try leaving your underripe tomatoes on the windowsill so they can soak up some sun

DO THIS STUFF

Preheat the oven to 200°C/180°C fan/400°F/gas mark 6.

Place the tomatoes in a colander set over a bowl and sprinkle with 1 teaspoon of salt. Toss to coat. Set aside at room temperature for a minimum of 15 minutes, tossing occasionally. The tomato juice will drip into the bowl.

Meanwhile, put the ripped loaf and Tofoo into a deep roasting tin. Drizzle with 2 tablespoons of the oil and toss until covered. Bake for about 25 minutes or until crisp. Remove from the oven and leave to cool.

Place the colander of tomatoes on a plate. Add the shallot, garlic, mustard and vinegar to the bowl of tomato juice. Add the remaining oil, whisking constantly.

Combine the toasted bread and Tofoo, tomatoes and dressing in a large bowl. Add the basil leaves and toss everything to coat and season to taste. Set aside to allow the flavours to absorb for at least 30 minutes, the longer the better, until the dressing is completely absorbed by the bread. Serve, preferably basking in sunshine.

WHY NOT TRY:

Adding a chopped red onion or spring onion.

CORONATION TOFOO SALAD

Embrace this retro royal dish made with handy storecupboard ingredients. It's tasty on its own, and perfect as a sandwich filling or piled high on a baked potato.

Serves: **4**
Preparation: **5 MINUTES**
Cooking: **10 MINUTES**

GET THIS STUFF

2 tbsp medium curry powder
1 tbsp sunflower oil
1 x 225g pack Smoked Tofoo, drained, dried and crumbled
150g mayonnaise
1 tbsp cashew butter
zest and juice of 1 lime
8 dried apricots, finely chopped
2 tbsp mango chutney
handful of fresh coriander, chopped
4 spring onions, sliced
2 tbsp toasted flaked almonds

DO THIS STUFF

Mix together half the curry powder and half the sunflower oil. Add the Tofoo and mix well.

Heat the remaining oil in a frying pan over a medium heat and cook the Tofoo for 7–10 minutes, turning regulary for an even golden brown. Remove from the pan with a slotted spoon and set aside to cool.

Mix together the mayonnaise, remaining curry powder, cashew butter, lime zest and juice, dried apricots and mango chutney. Stir through the Tofoo. Sprinkle with the spring onions and almonds. Serve with rice or as a filling for a sandwich or baked potato.

WHY NOT TRY:

· Adding a finely chopped red chilli for an extra kick.
· Serving piled on a baked sweet potato for a delicious lunch.

SMOKED TOFOO NOODLE SALAD

This salad can be prepared the night before, which makes it a perfect packed lunch. To keep the vegetables crunchy, layer them in the correct order. Dressing first, followed by noodles, then the firmer vegetables and protein, and finally top with the salad leaves.

Serves: **2**
Preparation: **20 MINUTES**
Cooking: **10 MINUTES**

GET THIS STUFF

1 tbsp sunflower oil
½ x 225g pack Smoked Tofoo, drained, dried and cut into 1.5cm cubes
85g fine egg noodles
100g broccoli, cut into small florets
1 carrot, peeled or scrubbed, grated
50g frozen edamame beans, defrosted in boiling water
2 tbsp sweetcorn, canned or defrosted
2 spring onions, chopped
handful mixed salad leaves

DO THIS STUFF

Heat the sunflower oil in a frying pan over a medium heat. When the oil is hot, add the Tofoo and cook for 5–7 minutes on each side until golden brown. Remove from the pan and leave to cool.

To make the cashew butter dressing, whisk all the ingredients together until smooth and creamy. Stir in 3–4 tablespoons of water to loosen it to a pouring consistency. Pour the dressing into the bottom of two jars with lids.

Cook the egg noodles following the pack instructions. Drain and cool.

Steam the broccoli in a steamer basket or colander placed over a pan of simmering water for about 3 minutes, until just tender and still bright green. You could also cook the broccoli in the microwave for 3–4 minutes.

Put the noodles in the jar on top of the dressing. Layer with the carrots, broccoli and Tofoo. Followed by the edamame beans, sweetcorn, spring onions and the salad leaves.

When you are ready to serve, tip the salad out and the dressing will start coating all the ingredients. Toss gently before eating.

For the cashew butter dressing
2 tbsp cashew butter
1 garlic clove, crushed
1 tbsp light soy sauce
2 tsp sunflower oil
2 tsp rice wine vinegar
pinch of dried chilli flakes

WHY NOT TRY:

· Using uncooked Smoked Tofoo if preferred.
· Swapping in peanut or almond butter for the dressing.
· Adding a layer of courgette or cucumber ribbons.

TOFOO SUSHI ROLLS

Sushi rolls, or *makizushi* in Japanese, are what most people think of when they think of sushi. *Makizushi* are made by wrapping up filling in rice and nori seaweed. Master the art and get creative with your fillings.

Serves: **2-4**

Preparation: **30 MINUTES**

GET THIS STUFF

250g sushi rice
1 tbsp rice wine vinegar
1 tsp caster sugar
3 sheets of nori seaweed, cut in half in the same direction as the lines on the nori
2 spring onions, finely chopped
wasabi paste (optional)
3 tbsp mayonnaise
¼ cucumber, cut into matchsticks
1 x 225g pack Smoked Tofoo, drained, dried and cut into 0.5cm strips

To serve
dark soy sauce
pickled sushi ginger

DO THIS STUFF

Cook the sushi rice following the pack instructions.

Mix together the rice wine vinegar and sugar and stir until the sugar dissolves.

Tip the rice into a large bowl and fluff with a fork, pour over the rice wine vinegar mixture and stir so that the rice is completely coated.

Place a piece of nori on a sheet of clingfilm or a sushi-making mat. Spoon over one-sixth of the rice and, with clean, damp fingers, press the rice over the nori, leaving a 1cm gap along one of the long sides. The rice layer should be thin and even. Spread a little wasabi (if using) in a line along the centre of the rice. Be careful not to add too much, it is powerfully hot stuff!

Spread over some mayonnaise. Top with a line of cucumber and Tofoo. Dampen the nori that isn't covered in rice and roll up from the rice side, pressing together. Repeat with the remaining nori and filling.

Slice the sushi rolls into 5–6 pieces with a wet serrated knife. Serve with soy sauce for dipping and some pickled ginger.

WHY NOT TRY:

· Stirring a few drops of hot chilli sauce into the mayonnaise.
· Adding a few strips of avocado to the line-up.

SAFFRON & LEMON TOFOO SALAD

This delicious combination was inspired by the Middle Eastern flavours of saffron, lemon and yoghurt. An elegant salad full of fragrant flavours that is sure to impress guests.

Serves: **2**
Preparation: **45 MINUTES**
Cooking: **15 MINUTES**

GET THIS STUFF

2 tbsp sunflower oil
1 x 280g pack Naked Tofoo, drained, dried and cut into 1.5cm cubes
Handful of salad leaves
½ cucumber, finely sliced
2 carrots, peeled and scrubbed, cut into ribbons
1 beetroot, peeled and finely sliced

For the marinade
1 tsp saffron strands
1 tsp ground turmeric
juice of 1 lemon and zest of ½
2 garlic cloves, finely chopped
¼ tsp salt
2 tbsp Greek or coconut yoghurt
2 tbsp olive oil

DO THIS STUFF

Grind the saffron in a pestle and mortar and then mix together with 2 tablespoons of water and the rest of the marinade ingredients. Add the Tofoo to the marinade and rub the marinade generously around the cubes of Tofoo. Cover and leave to marinate in the fridge for at least 30 minutes.

Remove the Tofoo from the marinade, reserving the marinade to use as a dressing.

Heat the sunflower oil in a large frying pan over a medium heat. Add the Tofoo and cook for 10 minutes, turning regulary until golden brown and crispy. Remove from the pan and drain on kitchen paper.

Pile the salad leaves in a large serving dish. Scatter over the cucumber, carrot ribbons and beetroot. Top with the Tofoo and drizzle with the reserved marinade.

WHY NOT TRY:

· Sprinkling with roasted walnuts or pistachios for added crunch.
· Adding a few sliced green olives for extra saltiness.

CITRUS TOFOO SLICES
with pomegranate couscous

This salad is chock-full of Middle Eastern flavours. If you make the couscous and marinate the Tofoo the day before, the dish will be even tastier (if that's possible).

GET THIS STUFF

1 x 280g pack Naked Tofoo, drained, dried and cut into 8 slices

For the marinade
juice of 1 lemon
2 tsp maple syrup
1 tbsp light soy sauce
3 tbsp za'atar, plus extra to serve

For the couscous
200g couscous
250ml vegetable stock
6 tbsp olive oil
juice of 1 orange
4 tbsp pomegranate seeds, plus a few extra to serve
3 tbsp mint, chopped
3 tbsp coriander, chopped
sea salt and freshly ground black pepper

DO THIS STUFF

Combine all the marinade ingredients in a shallow dish. Lay out the Tofoo in a shallow bowl and pour over the marinade. Leave the Tofoo to marinate for 30 minutes, flipping over halfway through. For even better results, cover and marinate in the fridge overnight.

Place the couscous in a bowl. Pour over the boiling stock and mix in the olive oil and orange juice. Season with sea salt and freshly ground black pepper. Cover tightly with clingfilm and sit in a warm place for 5–10 minutes, or until the liquid has been absorbed. Remove the clingfilm and fluff the grains with a fork. Leave to cool completely.

Preheat the oven to 200°C/180°C fan/400°F/gas mark 6. Line a baking tray with baking paper.

Place the Tofoo on the baking tray and cook for 20–25 minutes, turning over halfway through cooking.

For the pomegranate dressing, whisk together the garlic, allspice, lemon juice, pomegranate molasses, olive oil and any remaining Tofoo marinade.

Serves: **4**
Preparation: **30 MINUTES**
Marinating: **30 MINUTES+**
Cooking: **25 MINUTES**

For the pomegranate dressing
1 garlic clove, crushed
½ tsp ground allspice
juice of ½ lemon
2 tbsp pomegranate molasses
4–5 tbsp extra virgin olive oil

Stir the pomegranate seeds and chopped herbs into the couscous.

Serve the Tofoo slices alongside the herby couscous with a generous drizzle of pomegranate dressing. Sprinkle with extra za'atar and pomegranate seeds.

Image on the next page

WHY NOT TRY:

· Mixing the Tofoo in with the couscous for a perfect packed lunch.
· Swapping out the couscous for quinoa, bulgur wheat or riced cauliflower.

CITRUS TOFOO SLICES WITH POMEGRANATE COUSCOUS

RED THAI NOODLE SOUP
with crispy Tofoo

Sambal oelek is a chilli sauce or paste made from a mixture of chilli peppers, shrimp paste, garlic, ginger, shallot, sugar and lime juice. If you can't find sambal oelek use sriracha or chilli paste.

Serves: **4**
Preparation: **10 MINUTES**
Cooking: **15 MINUTES**

GET THIS STUFF

2 tbsp coconut oil
1 x 280g pack Naked Tofoo, drained, dried and cut into 16 strips
2 garlic cloves, crushed
2cm piece of fresh ginger, peeled and finely chopped
3 tbsp Thai red curry paste
2 vegetable stock cubes
500ml boiling water
1 x 400ml can coconut milk
2 tbsp dark soy sauce
2 tsp sambal oelek (optional)
1 red pepper, deseeded and chopped
200g instant wide rice noodles
2 spring onions, shredded

To serve
black sesame seeds
4 x handful of fresh coriander
lime wedges

DO THIS STUFF

Dry each strip of Tofoo well with kitchen paper. Heat half the coconut oil in a large pan over a medium heat. When the oil is hot, add the Tofoo and cook without stirring for about 2 minutes before turning over and cooking for a further 2 minutes until lightly golden and crispy on all sides.

Meanwhile, in a large pan, heat the remaining coconut oil and add the garlic and ginger. Cook for 1 minute, then add the red curry paste and cook for a further 1 minute, stirring constantly.

Add the stock cubes, boiling water, coconut milk, soy sauce, sambal oelek (if using) and the red pepper. Simmer for 5 minutes. Add the noodles and cook for a further 3 minutes, or until the noodles are cooked.

Assemble the soup by twisting some noodles in the bottom of each serving bowl. Add the Tofoo and spring onions. Pour over the broth, sprinkle with sesame seeds and top with a generous handful of coriander and a lime wedge.

WHY NOT TRY:

Using thin rice noodles or even cooked rice instead of the wide noodles.

TOFOO & MUSHROOM SOUP

You can use any mushrooms for this recipe, but dried mushrooms will give you extra depth of flavour and a bit more oomph.

Serves: **4**
Preparation: **15 MINUTES**
Soaking: **30 MINUTES**
Cooking: **20 MINUTES**

GET THIS STUFF

20g dried mushrooms
1 tbsp sunflower oil
1 garlic clove, very thinly sliced
3 large mushrooms, wiped and sliced
1 tsp Chinese rice wine
1 litre vegetable stock
1 tsp light soy sauce
½ tsp caster sugar
pinch of chilli flakes
1 x 225g pack Smoked Tofoo, drained, dried and diced
100g spinach leaves
1 tsp toasted sesame oil
4 spring onions, shredded
sea salt and freshly ground black pepper

DO THIS STUFF

In a small bowl, just cover the dried mushrooms in boiling water and soak for 20–30 minutes until softened.

Heat the oil in a large pan over a medium-high heat. Add the garlic and stir for a few seconds. Add the sliced mushrooms and cook for 1 minute.

Drain the dried mushrooms, reserving the soaking liquid. Add the soaked mushrooms and rice wine to the pan and cook for about 5 minutes until most of the liquid has evaporated.

Add the vegetable stock, soy sauce, sugar, chilli flakes and some black pepper. Bring to the boil and simmer, uncovered, for 10 minutes. Taste and adjust the seasoning.

Add the Tofoo and spinach leaves. Return to the boil and cook for 4 minutes until the spinach just wilts.

Remove from the heat, scatter in the spring onions and stir in the sesame oil. Serve immediately.

WHY NOT TRY:

· Experimenting with a variety of mushrooms such as shiitake, king oyster, enoki or shimeji.
· Adding instant noodles to the soup.

VIETNAMESE TOFOO SALAD

This light and refreshing salad combines all the flavours of Vietnam in one tasty bowl to blow the socks off your taste buds.

GET THIS STUFF

1 x 225g pack Smoked Tofoo, drained, dried and cut into 16 strips
2 tbsp cornflour
2 tbsp sunflower oil

For the dressing
2 red chillies, deseeded and chopped
3 garlic cloves, crushed and finely chopped
2 tbsp light brown sugar
juice of 1 large lime
1 tbsp fish sauce
3 tbsp olive oil

DO THIS STUFF

Put the dressing ingredients in a bowl or lidded jar and whisk or shake well. Set aside.

Pour boiling water over the noodles and leave to cook following the pack instructions. Drain the noodles into a colander and rinse well with cold water.

Transfer the drained noodles to a bowl and add the salad vegetables. Pour over the dressing and toss to coat all the ingredients.

Dry the Tofoo strips thoroughly with kitchen paper and toss in the cornflour.

Heat the sunflower oil in a frying pan over a medium heat and when hot add the Tofoo and cook for 7–10 minutes, turning until all the Tofoo strips are golden brown.

Serve the noodle salad topped with the Tofoo, a sprinkling of peanuts and a handful of coriander.

For the salad
200g rice noodles
2 carrots, peeled and
  scrubbed, cut into
  matchsticks
½ cucumber, deseeded
  and cut into matchsticks
¼ white cabbage, finely
  sliced
1 red pepper, deseeded
  and cut into matchsticks
4 radishes, finely sliced
4 tbsp chopped mint
4 tbsp roasted peanuts,
  chopped
small bunch of fresh
  coriander

WHY NOT TRY:

- Adding beansprouts to the salad.
- Using Thai basil instead of mint.
- Sprinkling with roasted pistachios instead of peanuts.

Image on the
next page

CRUNCHY TOFOO CAESAR SALAD

The breaded coating on the Tofoo gives you the crouton element of a traditional Caesar salad, but with even more flavour.

Serves: **4**
Preparation: **10 MINUTES**
Cooking: **15 MINUTES**

GET THIS STUFF

1 x 280g pack Naked Tofoo, drained, dried and cut into 8 slices
1 tbsp light soy sauce
4 tbsp cornflour
50g fresh breadcrumbs
generous pinch of sea salt
vegetable oil, for frying
3 heads of romaine lettuce
1 avocado, sliced
4 tbsp Caesar salad dressing
4 tbsp Parmesan cheese shavings

Try adding a handful of capers for a distinctive sour/salty flavour

DO THIS STUFF

Dry the Tofoo slices really well with kitchen paper. In a shallow bowl, cover the Tofoo slices with the soy sauce and leave for about 5 minutes.

When ready to cook the Tofoo, tip the cornflour into a shallow bowl. In another shallow bowl, mix the breadcrumbs with the salt.

Remove the Tofoo from the soy sauce and shake dry. Dip the Tofoo in the cornflour. Dip again in the soy, then coat in the breadcrumbs, pressing and turning until evenly coated.

Heat 2–3cm of oil in a deep frying pan over a medium heat. Place a piece of Tofoo into the oil, if it sizzles it is ready to start cooking. Carefully lower the Tofoo into the pan and cook for 2 minutes on each side until golden and crisp. You'll need to do this in batches as overcrowding the oil will stop the crumb getting crunchy. Remove and drain on kitchen paper.

To assemble the salad, slice the Tofoo into strips. Tear the romaine lettuce and add to a large mixing bowl. Top with the avocado and Tofoo slices. Drizzle with the Caesar dressing and cheese shavings.

WHY NOT TRY:

Sprinkling a handful of roasted chickpeas over the top for added crunch.

TOFOO GREEN SALAD

This simple, delicious salad celebrates spring freshness. You can add Tenderstem broccoli, green beans, peas or watercress for added green goodness. The more the merrier!

Serves: **4**
Preparation: **10 MINUTES**
Cooking: **5 MINUTES**

GET THIS STUFF

1 x quantity Tofoo halloumi (see page 200)
1 bunch of asparagus, trimmed
50g edamame beans
1 avocado, sliced
50g pea shoots
50g rocket
handful of basil leaves
handful of flat-leaf parsley
handful of mint
1 tbsp dill, chopped
1–2 tbsp extra virgin olive oil

DO THIS STUFF

Bring a large pan of water to the boil. Drop the asparagus into the boiling water and blanch for about 45 seconds. Remove the asparagus using a slotted spoon and immediately immerse in ice-cold water to stop it from cooking. Add the edamame beans to the pan and cook for 4–5 minutes. Drain and add to the asparagus. Drain the asparagus and beans, and pat dry.

Place asparagus, edamame beans, avocado, green leaves and herbs in a large serving dish.

Remove the Tofoo halloumi from the dressing and add to the salad. Mix the oil with the remaining Tofoo halloumi marinade and drizzle over the salad.

WHY NOT TRY:

· Celebrating spring by adding steamed Jersey Royals.
· Throwing a handful of freshly cut micro herbs over the salad just before serving.

TOFETA, WATERMELON & MINT SALAD

We can't believe that something this simple could be so delicious, but this is. Trust us. It's the perfect salad for a summer lunch in the garden.

Serves: **2-3**

Preparation: **10 MINUTES**
(plus 1 hour+ for the Tofeta)

GET THIS STUFF

¼ watermelon, cut into
    2cm cubes
½ cucumber, cut in half
    and sliced
½ x quantity Tofeta
    (see page 202)
handful of basil, torn
handful of mint, torn

For the dressing
3 tbsp maple syrup
juice of 1 lime
1 tbsp balsamic vinegar
large pinch of sea salt

DO THIS STUFF

Combine the watermelon, cucumber, Tofeta, basil and mint in a large bowl and gently toss together.

Whisk the dressing ingredients together and pour over the salad. Serve at room temperature or chilled.

Close your eyes and imagine you're in Greece for the ultimate experience!

WHY NOT TRY:

· Swapping the watermelon with a galia or honeydew melon or even a medley of melons.
· Sprinkling with roasted pecans.

TOFOO, SUPERFOOD & CRUNCHY SEEDS SALAD

This crunchy colourful salad is packed with goodness. The bigger the variety of vegetables of different colours, the brighter the bowl and all the more nutrients. Go wild!

Serves: **4**

Preparation: **20 MINUTES** (plus 1 hour+ for the Tofeta)

Cooking: **15 MINUTES**

GET THIS STUFF

1 x quantity Tofeta (see page 202)

For the salad

200g tender kale, trimmed and large stem removed

½ fennel bulb, finely shredded

⅓ red cabbage, finely sliced

1 orange, peeled and segmented

1 avocado, sliced

2 handfuls of rocket

For the crunchy seed topping

2 tsp olive oil, plus extra for greasing

100g mixed seeds, such as pumpkin, sunflower and/ or sesame

1 tbsp maple syrup

DO THIS STUFF

Preheat the oven to 200°C/180°C fan/400°F/gas mark 6. Lightly grease a baking tray with olive oil.

Mix together the mixed seeds, maple syrup and olive oil, and toss to combine. Press the mixture in an even layer (about 1cm thick) on the prepared baking tray and bake for 15 minutes or until golden brown. Leave to cool for at least 15 minutes before breaking into chunks.

Rip the kale into bite-sized pieces and add to a large serving dish. Add the fennel and red cabbage. Top with the orange segments, avocado and rocket. Top with the Tofeta and the Tofeta dressing and toss gently. Sprinkle with the crunchy seeds and serve.

WHY NOT TRY:

· Making double the quantity of the crunchy seeds and storing in a jar for a salad topping or as snacks.
· Having fun with the choice of vegetables – try adding cavolo nero, spinach or fine green beans or even apple or pear.

SMOKED TOFOO, GRAINS & BEETROOT BOWL

All you need is a pack of mixed grains in your storecupboard and some Tofoo in your fridge to rustle up a great, healthy meal in minutes. Here's a super tasty way to pull it all together.

Serves: **2**
Preparation: **15 MINUTES**
Cooking: **5 MINUTES**

GET THIS STUFF

1 x 250g pack microwave mixed grains
1 x 225g pack Smoked Tofoo, drained, dried and ripped into 2cm chunks
50g baby spinach, chopped
½ tsp cumin seeds
½ red onion, finely sliced
3 tbsp olive oil
1 tbsp lemon juice
1 tsp sugar
½ tsp Dijon mustard
4 tbsp hummus
100g cooked beetroot
1 tbsp chopped dill
sea salt and freshly ground black pepper

DO THIS STUFF

Heat the mixed grains following the pack instructions, then tip into a serving bowl. Add the Tofoo, spinach, cumin seeds and red onion.

Pour the olive oil, lemon juice, sugar and mustard into a screw-top jar, season and shake until well combined.

To serve, spoon the hummus into the bottom of two bowls, top with the mixed grain mixture and a scattering of beetroot. Drizzle with the lemon dressing and sprinkle with dill.

WHY NOT TRY:

· Swapping the Smoked Tofoo for a serving of Tofoo halloumi (see page 200).
· Adding a scattering of chopped walnuts for extra crunch.
· There are a variety of microwave grain pouches available – experiment until you find your favourite.

SMOKED TOFOO & PEACH IN A LEMON & PESTO DRESSING

You need ripe and ultra-juicy peaches for this recipe, so buy in plenty of time and ripen at home ready to make the salad. If you can't find ripe peaches, try nectarines, or leave unripe peaches in the sun to speed things up a little.

GET THIS STUFF

1 x 225g pack Smoked Tofoo, drained, dried and cut into 1cm slices
1–2 tbsp olive oil
15–20 fine asparagus spears
1 courgette, cut lengthways into long strips
mixed salad leaves
1 ripe peach, stoned and sliced
1 tbsp pine nuts
small handful of mint leaves

DO THIS STUFF

First, make the lemon and pesto dressing. Add the basil, garlic, pine nuts, lemon juice, nutritional yeast and some sea salt to a food processor and blend into a loose paste. Add the oil a little at a time and scrape down sides as needed. Season to taste.

Heat a griddle. Dry the Tofoo well with kitchen paper. Brush the Tofoo slices with oil and cook for 3–5 minutes on each side or until griddle marks appear. Remove from the griddle.

Brush the asparagus with the oil and place on the griddle. Cook for 2–3 minutes, turning a couple of times until griddle marks appear. Remove from the griddle.

Brush the courgettes with the oil and place the strips in a single layer on the griddle. Cook for 30 seconds–1 minute until griddle lines appear. If the courgette is peeled very thinly, there is no need to turn it over. If it's peeled a little thicker, turn it over and cook for a further 30 seconds on the other side. Remove from the griddle.

Serves: **4**

Preparation: **20 MINUTES**

Cooking: **20 MINUTES**

For the lemon & pesto dressing

100g basil leaves

1 garlic clove, roughly chopped

3 tbsp pine nuts

juice of 1 lemon

3 tbsp nutritional yeast

3–4 tbsp extra virgin olive oil

sea salt and freshly ground black pepper

Brush the peach with a little oil and griddle for 2 minutes on each side until griddle marks appear.

Divide the salad leaves between four plates and top with the Tofoo, asparagus, courgette and peach. Drizzle over the lemon and pesto dressing and sprinkle with pine nuts and mint.

Image on the next page

SMOKED TOFOO & PEACH IN A LEMON & PESTO DRESSING

4

Delicious Dinners

TOFOO BURGER

A good juicy burger is always a firm favourite in our kitchens. Pile this burger with your favourite topping, be it gherkins, cheese or coleslaw. The sky's the limit!

Serves: **2**
Preparation: **10 MINUTES**
Marinating: **1 HOUR**
Cooking: **25 MINUTES**

GET THIS STUFF

1 x 280g pack Naked Tofoo, drained and dried
3 tbsp sunflower oil
1 tbsp Dijon mustard, plus extra to serve
½ onion, sliced
2 burger buns, halved
2–3 tbsp mayonnaise
4 lettuce leaves, such as Little Gem
2 tomatoes, sliced
tomato ketchup, to serve

For the marinade
100ml light soy sauce
1 tbsp tomato purée
1 tbsp white miso paste
1 tbsp brown sauce

WHY NOT TRY:

Adding chilli flakes or sriracha to the marinade for a spicier burger.

DO THIS STUFF

Cut the Tofoo into two slabs, being careful not to break up the slabs. Pierce the Tofoo gently with a fork.

Whisk together all the marinade ingredients in a small bowl. Season well.

Place the Tofoo slabs in a shallow dish and pour over the marinade until covered. Transfer to the fridge for at least 1 hour.

Preheat the oven to 180°C/160°C fan/350°F/gas mark 4.

Heat a frying pan over a medium heat and add 2 tablespoons of oil. Put the Tofoo slabs in the pan and fry for 3 minutes. Turn over and fry for a further 3 minutes, then brush with half the mustard and turn and fry for a further 1 minute. Repeat on the other side.

Place the Tofoo burgers on a baking tray and bake in the oven for 15 minutes, brushing with the marinade halfway through cooking.

Meanwhile, add the remaining oil to the frying pan you used to cook the Tofoo and add the onions. Cook gently for about 10 minutes until soft and golden.

Toast the burger buns and start to build the burgers. Take the bun bottoms and spread with mayonnaise, top with the lettuce, sliced tomato and a Tofoo burger. Top with the fried onions. Serve with ketchup and extra mustard.

MASSAMAN TOFOO CURRY

Tofoo and potatoes cooked into a sweet, slightly spicy sauce. It's a flavour explosion!

Serves: **4**
Preparation: **10 MINUTES**
Cooking: **30 MINUTES**

GET THIS STUFF

2 tbsp coconut oil
1 x 400ml can coconut milk
4 tbsp Massaman curry paste
6 Charlotte potatoes, scrubbed and halved
4 kaffir lime leaves, plus extra to serve (optional)
150ml vegetable stock
150g green beans, trimmed
250g Naked Tofoo, drained, dried and cut into 2cm cubes
1 tbsp fish sauce
1 tbsp lime juice
½ tsp brown sugar

To serve
1 red chilli, deseeded and shredded
2 tbsp roasted peanuts
steamed jasmine rice

DO THIS STUFF

Heat the coconut oil in a large pan over a medium heat. Add 2 tablespoons of coconut milk and heat for a couple of minutes, then add the curry paste and cook for 2 minutes to release the flavours.

Add the remaining coconut milk, potatoes, lime leaves and stock. Bring to the boil and cook for 15 minutes or until the potatoes are just tender.

Add the green beans and Tofoo and reduce the heat to low. Cook for 10 minutes or until the beans are just cooked and the Tofoo has warmed though. Stir in the fish sauce, lime juice and sugar. Check seasoning to taste.

Serve the curry scattered with the red chilli, extra kaffir lime leaves (if using) and peanuts alongside steamed jasmine rice.

WHY NOT TRY:

· Adding carrots to the curry.
· Using potatoes left over from Sunday lunch.

CHIPOTLE TOFOO TACOS
with quick pickled onion & charred corn salsa

These tacos are great for a Mexican-inspired feast with friends, and are full of rich smoky flavours topped with a sharp, bright onion pickle.

Serves: **2**
Preparation: **15 MINUTES**
Cooking: **10 MINUTES**

GET THIS STUFF

100g Naked Tofoo, drained, dried and cut into 4 slices
1 tbsp sunflower oil
½ tsp chipotle paste
2 corn or wheat tortilla wraps
½ Little Gem lettuce
2 tsp hot sauce

For the quick pickled onion
½ red onion, sliced
1–2 tbsp white wine vinegar

For the charred corn salsa
2 tbsp sweetcorn, canned or scraped from the cob
½ red chilli, deseeded and diced
1 tomato, deseeded and diced
2 spring onions, sliced
2 sprigs of coriander, chopped
juice of ½ lime

DO THIS STUFF

For the pickled onion, place the sliced onion in a jar and cover with the white wine vinegar. Leave to pickle for at least 10 minutes.

To make the salsa, heat a dry pan over a medium heat and add the sweetcorn. Cook for 2–3 minutes until the corn is lightly charred. Add to a bowl along with the red chilli, tomato, spring onions and coriander. Toss all the ingredients together and add the lime juice, reserving a little to squeeze over the finished tacos before eating.

Heat a frying pan over a medium heat and add the oil. Add the Tofoo slices to the pan and fry for 4 minutes until golden. Turn over and fry for a further 3 minutes, then brush with the chipotle paste. Turn and fry for 1 minute.

Warm the tortillas in a dry pan over a medium heat for a few minutes.

To assemble the tacos, place the lettuce and Tofoo on to the tortillas, followed by the pickled red onion and charred corn salsa. Serve with a squeeze of lime juice and a drizzle of hot sauce. Wrap and eat.

WHY NOT TRY:

· Serving in crispy corn tacos shells for added crunch.
· Adding a spoonful of smashed avocado for extra richness.

TOFOO KIEV

A vegan twist on a classic – this Tofoo Kiev is filled with an irresistible garlic herby butter. Delicious!

GET THIS STUFF

2 x 280g pack Naked Tofoo, drained and dried
75g olive oil spread
1 tbsp roasted garlic purée
½ tsp white miso paste
1 tbsp flat-leaf parsley, finely chopped
½ tbsp chopped chives
vegetable oil, for shallow-frying
sea salt and freshly ground black pepper

For the crispy coating
50g cornflour
75g panko breadcrumbs
100ml soy or almond milk
60g plain flour

DO THIS STUFF

With an apple corer make a hole (about 2cm) through the middle of the Tofoo blocks (use a paring knife if you don't have an apple corer). Set aside the cored Tofoo for later.

Mix together the olive oil spread, garlic purée, miso and herbs. Mash with a fork until completely combined. Season well.

Take a 60cm length of clingfilm and fold it in half on a flat surface. Spoon the garlic spread mix on to the clingfilm in a line, then roll up the mixture aiming for a 2cm-wide roll. Twist the ends and transfer to the freezer for at least 30 minutes to harden.

Preheat the oven to 190°C/170°C fan/375°F/gas mark 5.

Season the cornflour and spread over a baking tray or large plate. Spread the breadcrumbs over another baking tray or large plate.

In a bowl, mix the milk slowly into the plain flour until you have a smooth batter about the thickness of double cream.

Unwrap the frozen garlic spread and cut a length slightly shorter than the Tofoo blocks. Insert into the Tofoo. Cover the filling at each end with the trimmed Tofoo corners.

Dry the Tofoo with kitchen paper and roll in the cornflour until it's completely covered, brushing off any excess. Now roll it in the batter, covering it completely. Finally, roll it in the panko breadcrumbs and set aside.

Heat about 2cm of vegetable oil in a large frying pan over a medium heat, add a small pinch of the loose panko crumbs and if they sizzle, then the oil is ready.

Carefully place the Tofoo Kievs into the oil and fry for 7–10 minutes. Gently turning the Tofoo with a pair of tongs until golden brown all over, including the ends.

Place the Kievs on a wire rack and then place the rack on a baking tray and bake in the oven for 15–20 minutes. Serve with greens and mash potatoes or oven chips.

Halve the Kiev and hear the crunch and watch that ooze!

WHY NOT TRY:

- Adding a few chilli flakes to the butter.
- Making double the quantity of the garlic butter and keeping it in the freezer to add to a juicy Tofoo steak.

TOFOO ROGAN JOSH

Rogan Josh is a sumptuous dish, full of flavour and spice. You can adapt the level of spice and heat to suit your taste, but we like it *hot*. Serve with rice or a nice warm naan.

Serves: **4**
Preparation: **20 MINUTES**
Marinating: **30 MINUTES**
Cooking: **30 MINUTES**

GET THIS STUFF

- 2 x 280g packs Naked Tofoo, drained, dried and cut into 2cm cubes
- 3 tsp ground turmeric
- 2 tbsp vegetable oil
- 1 medium onion, sliced
- 1 garlic clove, crushed
- 2cm piece of fresh ginger, peeled and grated
- 1 tsp ground cumin
- 1 tsp ground coriander
- 1 cinnamon stick
- 1 green cardamom pod, lightly crushed
- 3 cloves
- 1 red chilli, deseeded and diced
- 1 bay leaf
- 1 tbsp tomato purée
- 1 x 400g can chopped tomatoes
- 80g green beans
- 8 cherry tomatoes, halved

DO THIS STUFF

Toss the Tofoo in 2 teaspoons of turmeric and set aside for 30 minutes.

Heat the oil in a large pan and cook the onion over a gentle heat for 5 minutes until translucent.

Add the garlic, ginger and marinated Tofoo. Then add the dry spices, including the remaining turmeric, chilli and bay leaf. Cook for a few minutes, stirring to ensure the mixture doesn't stick.

Add the tomato purée, canned tomatoes and 100ml water. Cook over a low heat for 10 minutes, then add the green beans and cherry tomatoes. Season with salt and pepper and cook for a further 10 minutes.

You can add a little more water if the sauce is too thick!

Add the yoghurt, if using. Scatter with coriander leaves and serve with wedges of lime and rice or naan.

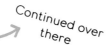

Continued over there

1 tbsp natural yoghurt
  (optional)
3–4 coriander sprigs
sea salt and freshly ground
  black pepper
lime wedges, to serve

WHY NOT TRY:

- Adding cubed aubergine, cauliflower or courgette for a chunkier curry.
- Serving with a slaw for added freshness.

PIRI-PIRI TOFOO PIZZA

A sneaky cheat with ready-made pizza bases makes this recipe a super quick dinner. Feel free to make your own bases if you're up for the challenge!

Serves: **2**
Preparation: **15 MINUTES**
Cooking: **15 MINUTES**

GET THIS STUFF

2 tbsp olive oil
2 garlic cloves, finely chopped
200ml passata
handful of fresh basil leaves
1 x 280g pack Naked Tofoo, drained and dried
1 tbsp piri-piri seasoning
2 ready-made pizza bases
1 red onion, sliced
1 yellow pepper, deseeded and sliced
1 red chilli, deseeded and sliced
80g mozzarella cheese, grated
sea salt and freshly ground black pepper
rocket, to serve

DO THIS STUFF

Preheat the oven to 220°C/200°C fan/425°F/gas mark 7.

Heat 1 tablespoon of oil in a large pan over a medium heat. Add the garlic and passata and cook for 3–5 minutes or until the passata has thickened slightly. Tear the basil and add to the sauce. Season to taste with salt and pepper.

Tear the Tofoo into chunks and toss with the piri-piri seasoning.

Spread the pizza bases with the sauce, then top with the Tofoo, onion, yellow pepper and chilli. Sprinkle over the cheese.

Place the pizzas on baking trays or directly on the oven rack and drizzle with the remaining olive oil. Bake in the oven for 8–10 minutes until the cheese has melted. Serve topped with a pile of rocket.

WHY NOT TRY:

· Making this pizza on a tortilla or a flatbread for a lighter alternative.
· Adding marinated artichokes.

TERIYAKI TOFOO

Sticky Teriyaki is a good staple dinner recipe and oh so moreish. This recipe is perfect for a quick weeknight supper for two.

Serves: **2**
Preparation: **10 MINUTES**
Marinating: **10 MINUTES**
Cooking: **10 MINUTES**

GET THIS STUFF

1 x 280g pack Naked Tofoo, drained, dried and cut into 3cm cubes
1 tbsp vegetable oil
1 red onion, sliced
1 red chilli, deseeded and sliced
150g mangetout
2 tsp sesame seeds

For the Teriyaki marinade
3 tbsp dark soy sauce
1 tbsp mirin
1 tbsp sesame oil
2 tbsp light brown sugar
2cm piece of fresh ginger, peeled and grated
2 garlic cloves, grated
1 tbsp cornflour

DO THIS STUFF

Mix together all the marinade ingredients in a bowl, add 100ml water and stir to combine. Add the Tofoo to the marinade and leave for at least 10 minutes.

Heat the oil in a frying pan over a medium heat and add the onion and chilli. Cook for 5 minutes until just beginning to soften.

Add the Tofoo and marinade to the pan and stir-fry, mixing well, for 5 minutes until the Tofoo is warmed through and the sauce has thickened.

Add the mangetout, stir and cook for a couple of minutes so that the mangetout is still crunchy.

Serve a sprinkling of sesame seeds and some rice alongside.

Psst, it's delicious in a stir-fry too!

WHY NOT TRY:

Making double the amount of marinade and storing it in the fridge for those last-minute dinners.

CRISPY TOFOO OK SAUCE

OK sauce is similar to brown sauce in both taste and appearance – fruity and delicious, it tastes *much* more than just okay.

Serves: **2**
Preparation: **10 MINUTES**
Cooking: **20 MINUTES**

GET THIS STUFF

vegetable oil, for shallow-frying
1 x 280 pack Naked Tofoo, drained, dried and cut into 1cm cubes
2 tbsp cornflour, plus 1 tsp for the sauce

For the OK sauce
2 garlic cloves, minced
1 tsp toasted sesame oil
1 tbsp rice vinegar
1 tbsp light brown sugar
2 tbsp sweet chilli sauce
2 tbsp tomato purée
1 tbsp light soy sauce

To serve
basmati rice
sliced red chillies

DO THIS STUFF

Heat about 2cm of oil in a deep frying pan over a medium heat. Dry the Tofoo well with kitchen paper and coat with the cornflour.

Once the oil is hot, add the coated Tofoo and shallow-fry for 7–10 minutes, turning over regulary until golden and crispy. You may need to do this in a couple of batches. Drain on kitchen paper and set aside.

Mix together all the ingredients for the OK sauce in a small bowl. Mix the 1 teaspoon of cornflour with a little water to make a thick paste. Add to the sauce and mix well.

Heat a wok or frying pan and add 1 tablespoon of oil. Add the OK sauce and heat gently until the sauce thickness slightly. If it suddenly becomes too thick, add a splash of water.

Add the crispy Tofoo and stir-fry together for 5 minutes until the Tofoo is coated in the sauce. Serve with basmati rice and sliced red chillies.

WHY NOT TRY:

· Adding Chinese 5 spice to the sauce for extra kick.
· Serving with noodles and stir-fried vegetables. Yum.

TOFOO PAD THAI

Tofoo is an amazing protein to add to a Pad Thai; it absorbs all the hot, zingy flavours and the texture complements the crunchy peanuts.

Serves: **2**
Preparation: **10 MINUTES**
Cooking: **10 MINUTES**

GET THIS STUFF

100g dried flat rice noodles
1 tbsp vegetable oil
1 shallot, thinly sliced
1 red chilli, deseeded and sliced
1 x 280g pack Naked Tofoo, drained, dried and diced
2 garlic cloves, crushed
2 tsp tamarind paste
2 tbsp fish sauce
juice of 1 lime
1 tbsp muscovado sugar
6 spring onions, sliced
150g beansprouts
½ tsp toasted sesame oil

To serve
50g salted peanuts, crushed
handful of coriander leaves
1 spring onion, shredded
1 lime, halved

DO THIS STUFF

Cook the noodles following the pack instructions. Drain and set aside.

Heat a wok or frying pan over a medium heat and add the oil. Add the shallot and chilli and cook for a couple of minutes. Add the Tofoo and cook for 7 minutes until golden brown. Add the garlic and cook for 2 minutes.

Stir in the cooked noodles, tamarind paste, fish sauce, lime juice and sugar. Stir-fry, tossing the noodles until mixed well. Chopsticks work well to stir as they help to break up any clumps of noodles.

Add the spring onions and beansprouts, mixing well. Cook for a couple of minutes until the beansprouts have warmed through. Drizzle with the sesame oil.

Serve with a sprinkling of crushed peanuts, coriander, spring onion and a squeeze of lime.

WHY NOT TRY:

· Adding extra vegetables, such as green beans or mangetout.
· Using Tofoo scrambled egg (see page 26) for a more authentic Pad Thai experience.

TOFOO KATSU

This fragrant Japanese-style curry sauce is a perfect partner for the crispy Tofoo. You can make the sauce ahead and even freeze it for a quick midweek meal.

GET THIS STUFF

2 x 280g packs Naked Tofoo, drained, dried and each block sliced into 6 pieces
75g plain flour
the drained water from 1 x 400g can chickpeas
200g panko breadcrumbs
2–4 tbsp vegetable oil
basmati rice, to serve

DO THIS STUFF

For the katsu sauce, heat the oil in a large pan. Add the onions and cook for 4–5 minutes or until just beginning to soften. Add the carrots, garlic and ginger, and reduce the heat to low to avoid the garlic burning. Cook for 4-5 minutes until all the vegetables are soft.

Add the turmeric and curry powder and cook over a low-medium heat until fragrant.

Add the flour to the pan, stir and cook for 2 minutes. Slowly add the stock, little by little, stirring as you go until you get a smooth sauce. Stir in the coconut milk. Add the soy sauce and sugar to taste. Simmer for 5 minutes. Leave to cool slightly and strain through a sieve to make it super smooth. You can also blitz the sauce with a blender for a really smooth texture. Set aside.

Dry each slice of Tofoo very well with kitchen paper. Set out three shallow bowls. Add the flour to one. Pour the water from the tin of chickpeas into the next. Whisk the chickpea water until it is white and fluffy. Finally, add the panko breadcrumbs to the third.

Dip the Tofoo in the flour, then the chickpea water froth, then the panko breadcrumbs.

For the katsu sauce

2 tbsp vegetable oil
2 onions, finely chopped
2 carrots, peeled and diced
2 garlic cloves, crushed
4cm piece of fresh ginger,
    peeled and grated
2 tsp ground turmeric
4 heaped tbsp mild curry
    powder
2 tbsp plain flour
600ml vegetable stock
200ml coconut milk
2 tsp light soy sauce
2 tsp caster sugar, to taste

Pour the remaining vegetable oil into a deep frying pan over a medium heat. Once hot, add the Tofoo in batches. Cook for about 3–4 minutes until golden brown on one side. Turn over and cook for a further 3–4 minutes or until golden brown.

Serve the Tofoo alongside steaming rice with a generous covering of the hot katsu sauce. Tuck in!

Image on the
next page

WHY NOT TRY:

· Using soy sauce instead of chickpea water.
· Serving with a sharp vegetable pickle such as pickled onion
  or radish.

JERK SMOKED TOFOO
with pineapple salsa & coconut rice

The combination of creamy coconut rice, spicy jerk seasoning and fruity salsa is the perfect way to bring some Caribbean sunshine to your dinner table.

Serves: **2**
Preparation: **15 MINUTES**
Cooking: **20 MINUTES**

GET THIS STUFF

120g basmati rice
1 x 400ml can coconut milk
1 x 225g pack Smoked
   Tofoo, drained, dried
   and cut into 6 slices
2 tsp jerk seasoning
1 tbsp sunflower oil

For the pineapple salsa
200g pineapple, finely
   chopped
1 red pepper, deseeded
   and finely chopped
4 spring onions, sliced
handful of mint leaves
zest and juice of 1 lime

DO THIS STUFF

Rinse the rice in a sieve under cold water until the water runs clear. Put the rice in a saucepan and add the coconut milk and 50ml water. Bring to the boil, stirring occasionally so that the rice doesn't stick to the bottom. Once the liquid is boiling, cover and reduce the heat to the lowest setting and steam for 15 minutes until all the liquid has evaporated and the rice is cooked through.

For the salsa, mix together the pineapple, red pepper and spring onions. Add the mint, lime zest and juice, stir and leave to sit while you cook the Tofoo.

Dry the Tofoo slices well with kitchen paper and rub each Tofoo slice with the jerk seasoning. Heat a frying pan over a medium heat and add the oil. Fry the Tofoo slices for 4–5 minutes until the slices are beginning to turn golden brown, but the seasoning has not burnt.

Serve the jerk Tofoo with the pineapple salsa and coconut rice.

WHY NOT TRY:

· Griddling the pineapple before chopping for added sweetness.
· Adding chopped red chilli to give the salsa an extra kick.
· Swapping jerk seasoning for Cajun seasoning.

SMOKED TOFOO FINGERS IN SATAY SAUCE

The crunch of the Tofoo here is a match made in heaven with the tangy peanut sauce. Serve with rice, noodles or in a wrap. Thank us later.

Serves: **2**
Preparation: **10 MINUTES**
Cooking: **10 MINUTES**

GET THIS STUFF

juice of 2 limes
3 tbsp dark soy sauce
2 tbsp sriracha
1 x 225g pack Smoked Tofoo, drained, dried and cut into 6 long strips
4 tbsp cornflour
1 tbsp coconut oil
150g crunchy peanut butter
150ml coconut milk
50g roasted peanuts, crushed
2 spring onions, shredded

To serve
steamed rice
coriander leaves
lime wedges

DO THIS STUFF

Mix together half the lime juice, 2 tablespoons of soy sauce and the sriracha and pour over the Tofoo. If time allows, leave to stand for 30 minutes.

When ready to cook, put the cornflour in a small bowl and dip the Tofoo in the cornflour until completely covered.

Heat the coconut oil in a frying pan over a medium heat. Add the Tofoo fingers and fry on all sides for 3–4 minutes per side, until golden and crispy. Remove from the pan and drain on kitchen paper.

Mix together the peanut butter, coconut milk, the remaining soy sauce and lime juice in a small pan. Add any remaining marinade from the Tofoo, heat and stir until all the ingredients are well combined. Add a splash of water to loosen if the sauce is a little thick.

Serve the Tofoo drizzled with the sauce and sprinkled with crushed peanuts and shredded spring onions. Serve with rice, coriander leaves and lime wedges.

WHY NOT TRY:

· Spearing the marinated Tofoo on to skewers and adding vegetables like pepper or courgettes for an added crunch.
· Sprinkling the skewers with chopped chilli or chilli flakes.

SWEET & SOUR TOFOO

Make this takeaway favourite a fakeaway feast at home. Chunks of crisp Tofoo in a delicious but simple sweet and sour sauce. You had us at 'Tofoo'.

Serves: **4**
Preparation: **10 MINUTES**
Cooking: **12 MINUTES**

GET THIS STUFF

1 x 280g pack Naked Tofoo, drained, dried and cut into 2cm cubes
6 tbsp cornflour
vegetable oil, for frying
227g can pineapple in juice
2 tbsp cider vinegar
2 tbsp dark soy sauce
1 tbsp clear honey
2 tbsp tomato ketchup
1 level tbsp cornflour
1 red pepper, deseeded and sliced
1 yellow pepper, deseeded and sliced
150g carrots, peeled and cut into batons
125g mangetout, halved
3 spring onions, sliced diagonally, plus extra to serve
rice, to serve

DO THIS STUFF

Dry each cube of Tofoo really well with kitchen paper. Place 4 tablespoons of cornflour in a small bowl. Dip each Tofoo cube in the cornflour, making sure to cover the cubes completely.

Add 2cm of vegetable oil to a wok or large frying pan over a medium heat. Add the Tofoo and fry for 10–12 minutes, turning regulary until evenly golden brown. Remove from the pan and drain on kitchen paper. Wipe the wok or frying pan clean.

Drain the pineapple into a small bowl, reserving the juice. Cut the pineapple into bite-sized pieces and set aside. Add the vinegar, soy sauce, honey and ketchup to the juice. Mix the remaining cornflour with 2 tablespoons of cold water and add to the bowl with the juice.

Heat 2 tablespoons of oil in the wok or large frying pan and add the peppers and carrots. Stir-fry for 3 minutes. Add the mangetout, spring onions and pineapple and stir-fry for 30 seconds.

Pour in the sauce and stir until simmering. Simmer for 1–2 minutes until the sauce is thick and glossy. Add the Tofoo and stir until covered in the sauce.

Serve on a bed of rice with a sprinkling of spring onions.

WHY NOT TRY:

Adding extra vegetables such as courgettes or green beans.

SMOKED TOFOO CARBONARA

This rich, creamy, smoky pasta is a fresh take on an Italian classic. What's not to like? *Bellissima!*

Serves: **2**
Preparation: **10 MINUTES**
Cooking: **25 MINUTES**

GET THIS STUFF

200g spaghetti
1 tbsp olive oil
4 shallots, finely chopped
3 garlic cloves, crushed
1 x 225g pack Smoked Tofoo, drained, diced and dried with kitchen paper
8 chestnut mushrooms, wiped and sliced
150ml white wine
150ml single cream
sea salt and freshly ground black pepper

To serve
grated Parmesan cheese
handful of flat-leaf parsley, chopped

DO THIS STUFF

Bring a saucepan of water to the boil. Add the spaghetti and cook following the pack instructions. Drain.

Meanwhile, heat a frying pan over a medium heat and add the olive oil. Add the shallots and cook for 5 minutes until just softened. Add the garlic and Tofoo and continue frying for 5 minutes until the Tofoo is lightly golden brown.

Add the mushrooms and cook for 5 minutes until the mushrooms are lightly browned and all the moisture has evaporated. Pour in the wine and boil for 3–5 minutes or until the white wine has reduced by half.

Add the single cream, reduce the heat to low and cook for 3–5 minutes to thicken the sauce. Season to taste with salt and pepper.

Add the drained pasta to the sauce and mix well. Serve the carbonara with a grating of Parmesan and a sprinkling of parsley.

WHY NOT TRY:

· Adding chopped Tofoo bacon (see page 21) on top.
· Stirring in a couple of tablespoons of frozen peas.

TOFOO SPAGHETTI BOLOGNESE

There are not many people that don't have a big ol' soft spot for a hearty bowl of spag bol. This version won't disappoint, we promise.

Serves: **2**
Preparation: **15 MINUTES**
Cooking: **1 HOUR 10 MINUTES**

GET THIS STUFF

2 tbsp nutritional yeast
1 tbsp dark soy sauce
3 tbsp olive oil
1 x 280g pack Naked Tofoo, drained, dried and crumbled

For the tomato sauce
1 onion, diced
2 carrots, peeled and finely chopped
2 celery sticks, diced
2–3 garlic cloves, finely chopped
2 x 400g cans chopped tomatoes
1 tbsp tomato purée
1 tbsp dried oregano
1 tbsp brown sugar
sea salt and freshly ground black pepper

To serve
450g cooked spaghetti
4 tbsp Parmesan cheese, grated
handful of basil leaves, torn

DO THIS STUFF

Heat 2 tablespoons of oil in a large pan over a medium heat. Add the onion, carrots and celery and cook for 5–7 minutes until the vegetables are beginning to soften. Add the garlic and cook for a further 2 minutes. Pour in the tomatoes, then add the tomato purée, half a can of water, the oregano and sugar. Bring to the boil, then reduce the heat and continue to simmer for 45 minutes–1 hour until the vegetables are soft. Add more water if the sauce becomes too thick.

Meanwhile, preheat the oven to 200°C/180°C fan/400°F/gas mark 6.

Mix the nutritional yeast, soy sauce and olive oil together in a large bowl. Stir in the crumbled Tofoo, making sure all of the Tofoo is evenly coated.

Spread the Tofoo evenly over a baking dish. Bake for about 45 minutes, stirring the Tofoo every now and again. The Tofoo should be nice and browned. The smaller crumbles will be darker than the larger crumbles, but that's fine because it will provide a variety of textures. Keep a close eye on it towards the end of cooking so that it doesn't overcook and become tough.

Stir the Tofoo into the tomato sauce and continue to cook for a further 10 minutes. This will allow the Tofoo to absorb the sauce and get gloriously chewy. Serve on a bed of spaghetti topped with grated Parmesan and a scattering of basil.

CHAR SIU TOFOO NOODLES

Char siu literally means 'fork roast' – 'char' being 'fork' and 'siu' being 'roast' after the traditional cooking method for the dish. We've taken the essence of that traditional dish to make this delicious noodle dish with oodles of flavour.

Serves: **2**
Preparation: **15 MINUTES**
Marinating: **30 MINUTES**
Cooking: **10 MINUTES**

GET THIS STUFF

- 1 x 280g pack Naked Tofoo, drained, dried and cut into 1cm-thick strips
- 2 tbsp cornflour
- 2 tbsp vegetable oil
- 300g ready-cooked noodles, such as udon
- 200g choy sum, washed and sliced
- 2 tbsp sesame seeds, toasted

For the char siu sauce
- 4 tbsp hoisin sauce
- 3 tbsp maple syrup
- 3 tbsp dark soy sauce
- 3 tbsp dry sherry
- 1 tsp Chinese 5 spice
- 1 tsp toasted sesame oil

DO THIS STUFF

Mix together all the char siu sauce ingredients. Put the Tofoo in a shallow bowl and add half the char siu sauce. Cover and refrigerate for at least 30 minutes, longer if possible.

When ready to cook the Tofoo, toss the marinated Tofoo strips in the cornflour.

Heat a deep frying pan over a medium heat and add the oil. When the oil is hot enough, add the Tofoo strips and fry for 3–4 minutes each side until golden. Transfer to a plate lined with kitchen paper.

Return the pan to the heat and add the noodles and choy sum and stir-fry for 3–4 minutes until well combined and warmed through. Add the Tofoo, pour over the remaining char siu sauce and heat through.

Serve sprinkled with the toasted sesame seeds.

WHY NOT TRY:

- Swapping choy sum for spring greens or Tenderstem broccoli.
- Serving with rice instead of the noodles.

ONE-PAN TOFOO BALLS IN TOMATO SAUCE

Delicious, easy, one pan – this dish ticks all the boxes and is a great one to have in your weeknight recipe repertoire. Perfect for a full stomach and a small washing-up pile.

Serves: **4**
Preparation: **20 MINUTES**
Chilling: **20+ MINUTES**
Cooking: **30 MINUTES**

GET THIS STUFF

1 x 280g pack Naked Tofoo, drained, dried and cubed
2 onions, finely chopped
50g walnuts
4 garlic cloves, finely chopped
1 tbsp dried oregano
50g breadcrumbs
2 tbsp nutritional yeast
2 tbsp cornflour
2 tbsp olive oil
1 red pepper, deseeded and chopped
1 courgette, chopped
200ml vegetable stock
1 x 400g can chopped tomatoes
sea salt and ground black pepper

To serve
pasta

DO THIS STUFF

Place the Tofoo, half the onions, the walnuts, half the garlic, half the oregano, the breadcrumbs and nutritional yeast in a food processor and blitz to a coarse paste. Season well with salt and pepper.

Roll the mixture by the hand into 12 ping pong balls. Chill the balls for at least 20 minutes.

Place the cornflour on a shallow plate. Roll the balls in the cornflour.

Heat the oil in a large frying pan over a medium heat. Add the balls and fry gently for 7–10 minutes, rolling the balls so they become an even golden brown. Once even in colour, remove from the pan and drain on kitchen paper.

Return the pan to the heat and add the remaining onion, the pepper and courgette along with the remaining garlic and oregano. Add the stock and simmer for 5 minutes.

Add the chopped tomatoes and check the seasoning. Simmer gently for 10 minutes or until the sauce thickens slightly. Add the Tofoo balls and simmer gently for 5 minutes. Serve with your favourite pasta.

WHY NOT TRY:

Adding chilli to the tomato sauce.

TOFISH & CHIPS

The crunch of the batter and the softness of the Tofoo make a dream team. Serve with creamy peas and chips for a great weekend dinner. Wrap it up in old newspaper for an authentic chippie experience.

GET THIS STUFF

For the Tofish

250g Naked Tofoo, drained, dried and cut into 4 slabs
1 tbsp plain flour, seasoned with salt and pepper
100g self-raising flour
1 tsp dried seaweed, crumbled (optional)
100ml ale
vegetable oil, for deep-frying

For the peas

300g frozen peas
3 tbsp crème fraîche

DO THIS STUFF

Preheat the oven to 200°C/180°C fan/400°F/gas mark 6.

Bring a large pan of lightly salted water to the boil and cook the potato chips for 5 minutes. Drain the potatoes and dry really well with kitchen paper. Toss in 4 tablespoons of olive oil. Spread out over a non-stick baking tray and cook in the oven for 30 minutes, turning halfway through cooking.

Meanwhile, cook the peas in a pan of boiling water for 5 minutes, drain well and tip into a food processor with the crème fraîche. Blitz until well combined. Alternatively, mash them together with a fork. Return to the pan and set aside.

Pat the Tofoo once more with kitchen paper until very dry. Dust with the seasoned plain flour. Mix together the self-raising flour and seaweed, if using, then slowly whisk in the ale. Whisk until the batter is smooth and creamy.

For the chips
800g potatoes, such as
    King Edward, peeled and
    cut into 1cm-wide chips
4 tbsp olive oil

To serve
lemon wedges

Heat about 8cm of oil in a saucepan pan to 180°C. (If you do not have a thermometer, add a square of bread to the oil, if it sizzles the oil is ready.) Take a piece of Tofoo and dip it in the batter to coat evenly, then carefully lower into the hot oil and cook for 2–3 minutes until golden and crispy. Repeat with the remaining three pieces.

Gently reheat the peas.

Serve the battered Tofish with chips and a spoonful of peas, and don't forget the lemon wedge for a squeeze of sharpness.

Image on the
next page

WHY NOT TRY:

- Cutting the Tofoo into fingers and making crispy goujons.
- Adding fresh mint to the peas.

TOFOO RED THAI CURRY

This fragrant dish is such a delight. It's loaded with flavour and is an absolute crowd-pleaser. Seconds, please!

Serves: **4**
Preparation: **20 MINUTES**
Cooking: **30 MINUTES**

GET THIS STUFF

250g Naked Tofoo, drained, dried, sliced into 8 and each slice cut in half into a triangle
2 tbsp cornflour
3 tbsp coconut oil
1 tbsp ginger paste
1 tbsp garlic paste
5–6 tbsp Thai red curry paste
1 small carrot, peeled and cut into small cubes
1 red pepper, deseeded and chopped
2 x 400ml cans coconut milk
2 tbsp fish sauce
1 tsp brown sugar
1 tbsp Thai basil
handful coriander, plus extra to serve

To serve
1 lime, cut into 8 wedges
sticky rice

DO THIS STUFF

Dry the Tofoo triangles really well with kitchen paper. Toss gently in the cornflour until completely coated.

Heat 2 tablespoons of coconut oil in a deep frying pan over a medium heat. When the oil is hot enough, add the Tofoo and cook for 8–10 minutes until all sides are completely browned and crispy. Remove the Tofoo and set aside to drain on kitchen paper.

Heat the remaining coconut oil in a large pan over a medium heat and add the ginger, garlic and Thai red curry pastes. Stir and cook for 3–5 minutes until fragrant. Stir in the carrot and red pepper.

Add the coconut milk and gently bring to the boil. Reduce the heat and simmer for 15 minutes or until the carrot is tender. Add half the fish sauce and a pinch of brown sugar. Taste and add more fish sauce and sugar to taste.

Add the Tofoo and simmer for 5 minutes. Add the Thai basil and half the coriander.

Spoon the curry into bowls, squeeze over the lime wedges and serve with sticky rice and topped with coriander.

WHY NOT TRY:

Adding broccoli to the curry.

STICKY GARLIC TOFOO

This dish is impossible not to love, just don't go trying to kiss anyone after you've eaten it. To get the most out of the sticky element, make sure you chill this in the fridge for at least 20 minutes.

Serves: **2**
Preparation: **20 MINUTES**
Chilling: **20+ MINUTES**
Cooking: **10 MINUTES**

GET THIS STUFF

2 tbsp toasted sesame oil
4 garlic cloves, finely minced
125ml hoisin sauce
2 tbsp dark soy sauce
1 x 280g pack Naked Tofoo, drained, dried and cut into 3cm cubes
4 spring onions, shredded

To serve
basmati rice
150g charred Tenderstem broccoli
2 tbsp sesame seeds

DO THIS STUFF

Heat half the sesame oil in a small pan over a medium heat. Add the garlic and cook for 1–2 minutes until just softened, do not colour or allow to burn. Add the hoisin and soy sauces. Add the Tofoo cubes and mix to make sure the Tofoo is coated with the sauce. Remove from the heat, leave to cool, then transfer to the fridge for at least 20 minutes or until the sauce is cold, thick and sticky.

When ready to serve the Tofoo, heat the remaining sesame oil in a frying pan over a medium heat, once hot add the Tofoo cubes in a single layer along with the sauce. Cook for 5 minutes, turning the Tofoo cubes so there's an even coating on all sides. Add the chopped spring onions at the last minute and stir through.

Serve the sticky Tofoo with rice, Tenderstem broccoli and a generous sprinkle of sesame seeds.

WHY NOT TRY:

Adding chopped red chilli to the sauce for extra heat.

TOFOO HASSELBACK VEGETABLE TRAYBAKE

You don't *have* to cut the vegetables into hasselback, but it'll let the dressing soak in properly and let's be honest, it looks cool.

Serves: **4**
Preparation: **20 MINUTES**
Cooking: **1 HOUR**

GET THIS STUFF

- 800g mixed root vegetables, such as carrots, parsnips and/or beetroots, trimmed and scrubbed
- 4 tbsp olive oil
- 2 x 280g packs Naked Tofoo, drained, dried and cut into 8
- 2 red onions, cut into wedges
- 2 courgettes, cut into large chunks
- 3 tbsp white miso paste
- 4 tbsp maple syrup
- 1 tsp chilli flakes
- zest and juice of 1 orange
- sea salt and freshly ground black pepper

DO THIS STUFF

Preheat the oven to 220°C/200°C fan/425°F/gas mark 7.

Using a sharp knife, make several cuts, 2mm apart, roughly two-thirds of the way through each of the root vegetables.*

Pour the oil into a roasting tin and heat in the oven for 5 minutes. Add the root vegetables, season with salt and pepper and roast for 20 minutes. Add the Tofoo, onions and courgettes and roast for a further 20 minutes.

In a small bowl, mix together the miso paste, maple syrup, chilli flakes and the orange zest and juice. Pour over the roasting Tofoo and vegetables. Shake to loosen and mix, then roast for a further 15 minutes until crisp and sticky. Season and serve.

* If you are not cutting the vegetables into hasselback, just cut into large cubes

WHY NOT TRY:

This tip for cutting hasselback vegetables: place two chopsticks or wooden spoon handles either side of the long side of the vegetables. Slice the vegetables into 2mm slices. The chopsticks will prevent you from cutting through the vegetable.

SMOKED TOFOO BARBECUE BURGERS
with herby sweet potato wedges

This is a proper, hearty barbecue-weather supper and the sweetness of the sauce and sweet potatoes works wonders with the smokiness of the Tofoo.

GET THIS STUFF

- 1 x 225g pack Smoked Tofoo, drained and dried
- 2 tbsp ready-made barbecue sauce
- 1 Little Gem lettuce, shredded
- 4 tbsp ready-made coleslaw
- 4 brioche buns, halved and lightly toasted

For the smashed avocado
- 1 avocado, halved
- juice of ½ lime
- 2 spring onions, finely chopped
- pinch of chilli flakes

DO THIS STUFF

Preheat the oven to 200°C/180°C fan/400°F/gas mark 6.

Scrub the potatoes and cut lengthways into chunky wedges. Place in a large bowl of water and swish around gently.

Mix the olive oil with the garlic powder, rosemary and seasoning.

Drain the sweet potatoes and dry really well. Spread the potatoes out on a large baking tray. Ideally the potatoes should be in a single layer with a little space between each wedge – use more than one tray if necessary. Pour the herby oil over the potatoes and mix well to ensure that each wedge is coated.

Bake for 40–50 minutes, turning halfway through cooking, until the wedges are soft inside and crispy and golden on the outside.

Slice the block of Tofoo in half lengthways, then use a 7cm cookie cutter to cut out four burgers. Brush with barbecue sauce and arrange the Tofoo burgers on a lined baking sheet. Bake for 8–10 minutes, flip and return to oven for a further 8–10 minutes.

Serves: **4**

Preparation: **20 MINUTES**

Cooking: **1 HOUR 10 MINUTES**

For the rosemary chips
4 large sweet potatoes
4 tbsp olive oil
2 tsp garlic powder
1 tbsp dried rosemary
sea salt and freshly ground
    black pepper

For the smashed avocado, split the avocado in half, remove the stone and spoon the flesh into a bowl. Add the lime juice, spring onions, chilli flakes, salt and black pepper. Mash with a fork to your desired consistency.

To assemble, generously spread the top and bottom of each bun with the smashed avocado. Add a Tofoo burger and lettuce, top with a dollop of coleslaw. Serve with the herby potato wedges alongside.

Image on the next page

WHY NOT TRY:

Using Teriyaki sauce instead of the barbecue sauce.

SMOKED TOFOO BARBECUE BURGERS WITH HERBY SWEET POTATO WEDGES

TOFOO ROAST

Our take on a Sunday classic. This makes for a festive centrepiece, full of autumnal flavours.

GET THIS STUFF

250g Naked Tofoo, drained and dried
10–15 whole cloves

For the marinade
60ml olive oil
60ml light soy sauce
2 tbsp maple syrup
1 tbsp liquid smoke (optional)
1 tsp mustard powder
1 tsp garlic powder
½ tsp freshly ground black pepper

DO THIS STUFF

Whisk together the marinade ingredients. Place Tofoo in a small bowl and pour over the marinade. Try to cover as much of the Tofoo as you can. Leave to marinate in the fridge for as long as you can, anywhere between 12–24 hours. Turn the Tofoo over a few times to ensure a good covering. The better the marinade covering, the tastier the finished dish.

When you are ready to roast the Tofoo, preheat the oven to 200°C/180°C fan/400°F/gas mark 6. Line a small baking dish just bigger than the Tofoo with baking paper.

Take a small, sharp knife and score the top of the Tofoo in a diamond pattern. Place a clove in the middle of each diamond.

Roast the Tofoo for 40 minutes–1 hour, keeping an eye on it after 40 minutes so that the edges do not become too dark.

While the Tofoo is roasting, make the glaze. Add all the glaze ingredients to a saucepan, heat gently and stir to combine and dissolve the sugar. Bring to a boil, reduce the heat and simmer for about 7 minutes or until reduced by about half into a thick, glossy glaze.

For the glaze
zest and juice of 1 orange
juice of 1 lemon
3 tbsp orange marmalade
1 tbsp olive oil
1 tsp mustard powder
¼ tsp ground allspice

Pour the glaze over the Tofoo. Return it to the oven and roast for a further 10–15 minutes until the glaze has thickened and is just starting to darken at the edges. Remove the roast Tofoo and place on a serving dish.

Pour the marinade and glaze into a small pan and heat gently. Serve as a sauce alongside the roast Tofoo.

Serve with festive vegetables, such as roast potatoes, whole roast carrots and pan-fried sprouts.

The perfect
Sunday lunch!

WHY NOT TRY:

· Adding a spoonful of whisky to the glaze. We won't tell if you don't!
· Adding sweet chilli sauce to the marinade for a gentle heat.
· Using pineapple juice in the marinade instead of the orange juice.

SMOKY TOFOO & SWEET POTATO CAKES

Roasty, toasty and super comforting cosy food.

GET THIS STUFF

1 sweet potato (200g), peeled and cut into small chunks
1 tbsp olive oil
1 onion, finely chopped
1 small red pepper, deseeded and chopped
1 garlic clove, crushed
1 tsp ground cumin
1 tsp smoked paprika
1 x 225g pack Smoked Tofoo, drained and dried
50g roasted cashews
1 tsp mustard powder
150ml soy or almond milk
75g plain flour
50g fresh or panko breadcrumbs
vegetable oil, for frying
sea salt and freshly ground black pepper
kale and apple salad, to serve

DO THIS STUFF

For the Tofoo cake, put the sweet potato in a microwavable bowl, cover with clingfilm and cook on high for 3 minutes. Shake and cook for a further 3 minutes until soft.

Heat the oil in a frying pan over a medium heat and fry the onion and red pepper for 5 minutes. Add the garlic and spices and cook for 2 minutes. Set aside to cool slightly.

Blitz the Tofoo and cashews on pulse in a blender; do not over-blitz. Add the cooled sweet potato, fried onion and pepper. Season and blitz again until just combined – do not over-blitz into a paste. Shape into eight cakes and place on a lined baking tray. Chill until ready to use.

Mix together the mustard powder and milk in one bowl. In another bowl, mix together the flour and breadcrumbs.

Dip each cake into the breadcrumb mixture, then into the milk mixture, then back into the breadcrumb mixture. Repeat to get a good covering on each cake.

Heat 2cm of vegetable oil in a large frying pan over a medium-high heat. Carefully add the patties and gently fry for about 2–3 minutes on each side until just golden brown and crispy. Drain on kitchen paper.

Serve with a crunchy kale and apple salad.

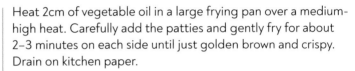

Image on the next page

WHY NOT TRY:

Adding chopped spinach to the patty mixture.

SMOKY TOFOO & SWEET POTATO CAKES

FILO TOFOO, SPINACH & PEPPER PIE

A very loose version of Greek spanakopita. The Tofoo and spinach are encased in layers of crispy filo pastry with added sharpness from the red peppers.

Serves: **6**
Preparation: **25 MINUTES**
Cooking: **40 MINUTES**

GET THIS STUFF

5 tbsp olive oil
1 onion, finely chopped
100g pine nuts
250g young spinach leaves
3 garlic cloves, crushed
1 x 280g pack Naked Tofoo, drained and dried
finely grated zest of 1 small lemon
40g fresh breadcrumbs
1 tsp dried oregano
3–4 tbsp finely chopped mint leaves
200g roasted red peppers from a jar, drained and sliced
sea salt and freshly ground black pepper
crisp green salad, to serve

For the pastry
7 sheets filo pastry (270g pack)
3 tbsp olive oil

DO THIS STUFF

Heat 2 tablespoons of oil in a large, deep frying pan over a medium heat. Add the onion and pine nuts and fry for 5 minutes, or until the onion has softened and the pine nuts are lightly browned, stirring regularly.

Place the spinach in a colander set over a large bowl. Pour over boiling water and shake dry. Squeeze the spinach with the back of a spoon to remove as much water as possible. Pat dry with kitchen paper and roughly chop.

Add the garlic and spinach to the pan with the onions.

Mash the Tofoo roughly with a fork in a large bowl. Roughly dry with kitchen paper, then add the lemon zest, breadcrumbs, oregano and mint. Season and mix well.

Preheat the oven to 200°C/180°C fan/400°F/gas mark 6.

Lay a sheet of baking paper slightly bigger than a filo sheet on a surface and brush with olive oil. Lay a sheet of filo on the paper and brush with olive oil. Lay another sheet of filo at 90 degrees across the first one and brush with olive oil. Lay the next at 45 degrees and brush with olive oil. Continue with the remaining filo sheets, creating a star effect. Use the paper to lift the pastry into a 23cm cake tin, allowing the excess filo to hang over the sides of the tin.

Continued on the next page

Spoon half the spinach mixture into the filo, top with the Tofoo mixture and then a layer of the red peppers. Top with the remaining spinach mixture.

Fold the overhanging filo over the top of the filling, scrunching to seal. Scrunch the remaining filo and use it to fill any gaps. It does not have to look neat and tidy. Brush the pastry with olive oil and sprinkle with black pepper.

Bake for 35 minutes, or until the pastry is crisp and golden brown and the filling is hot.

Leave to cool slightly before using the baking paper to ease the pie out of the tin.

Serve in slices with a crisp green salad.

WHY NOT TRY:

Adding a layer of griddled courgettes or grated cheese to the filling.

TOFOO & BUTTERNUT SQUASH RISOTTO

You can't rush a risotto; take the time, sip a big glass of wine and enjoy the process. It's worth it in the end.

Serves: **4**
Preparation: **15 MINUTES**
Cooking: **40 MINUTES**

GET THIS STUFF

1kg butternut squash, peeled and cut into bite-sized chunks
4 tbsp olive oil
1 x 280g pack Naked Tofoo, drained, dried and cut into 2cm cubes
1.5 litres vegetable stock
50g butter
1 onion, finely chopped
300g risotto rice
1 x 125ml glass white wine
bunch of sage, leaves picked, half left whole
50g hard cheese, finely grated
sea salt and freshly ground black pepper

WHY NOT TRY:

· Adding peas.
· Stirring in some nutritional yeast for extra cheesy flavour.

DO THIS STUFF

Preheat the oven to 220°C/200°C fan/425°F/gas mark 7.

Place the squash in a large roasting tin. Drizzle with 1 tablespoon of oil and roast for 10 minutes. Add the Tofoo, drizzle with another tablespoon of oil and season well. Roast for a further 20 minutes, turning the squash and Tofoo over to ensure even roasting.

Bring the stock to the boil and keep on a low simmer.

In a separate pan, melt half the butter with 1 tablespoon of olive oil over a medium heat. Stir in the onion and cook gently for 8–10 minutes until soft but not coloured.

Add the rice to the onion and stir to completely coat in the butter and oil until it is glossy.

Pour in the wine and simmer until evaporated. Reduce the heat, then add one ladle of stock at a time, stirring gently but constantly during each addition. When the stock has been absorbed, add another ladleful of stock. Continue until all the stock has been added and the rice is just cooked. This should take 20–25 minutes; the risotto should be creamy and slightly soupy. Season well.

Heat the remaining oil in a small pan over a medium heat and when hot add the whole sage leaves and cook for 1–2 minutes or until crisp. Remove with a slotted spoon and set aside on kitchen paper.

Once the risotto is cooked, stir in the Tofoo and squash, season and add the cheese and remaining butter. Serve the risotto topped with the crisp sage leaves.

TOFOO CHILLI WITH COURGETTI

This great chilli recipe is the ultimate dish to serve to friends for a casual get-together. You can double or even triple the quantities to feed a crowd.

Serves: **2**
Preparation: **15 MINUTES**
Cooking: **20 MINUTES**

GET THIS STUFF

1 tbsp olive oil
1 small onion, chopped
2 green chillies, deseeded and diced*
1 x 225g Smoked Tofoo, drained, dried and cut into 2cm cubes
1 garlic clove, finely chopped
1 red pepper, deseeded and finely chopped
100g button mushrooms, wiped and halved
2 tbsp sun-dried tomato purée
1 x 227g can chopped tomatoes
100ml boiling water
1 x 225g can kidney beans, drained and rinsed
20g dark chocolate (70% cocoa solids)
200g courgettes
sea salt and freshly ground black pepper

DO THIS STUFF

Heat the oil in a deep frying pan over a medium heat and add the onion and chillies. Cook for 5 minutes until the onion starts to soften. Add the Tofoo, garlic, red pepper and mushrooms and stir-fry for 5 minutes.

Stir in the tomato purée and chopped tomatoes along with the boiling water, cover and simmer for 15 minutes, stirring occasionally.

Add the beans and chocolate and stir until chocolate melts. Season well with salt and pepper.

Spiralise the courgettes and steam for 5 minutes or cook in a large pan of water for 2 minutes. Drain well.

Divide the courgettes between two warmed serving plates and top with the chilli. Dollop over the yoghurt and sprinkle with coriander to serve.

*(only use one if you don't want it hot)

WHY NOT TRY:

· Serving with spaghetti, rice or even in a jacket potato for some carb action!
· Adding other beans such as black beans or pinto beans as well or instead of the kidney beans.
· Doubling the quantity and serving it for a winter gathering or Halloween party.
· Make double and freeze half for a quick, winter warmer dinner.

CRISPY TOFOO IN SPICY TOMATO PASTA SAUCE

Pasta and tomato sauce is a staple in just about every household but adding some crispy Tofoo makes it into something a little special that'll always hit the spot.

Serves: **4**
Preparation: **10 MINUTES**
Cooking: **30 MINUTES**

GET THIS STUFF

2 tsp cornflour
1 tsp ground turmeric
1 tbsp olive oil
1 x 280g pack Naked Tofoo, drained, dried and roughly torn into about 2cm pieces

For the tomato sauce
2 tbsp olive oil
1 onion, finely chopped
2 garlic cloves, crushed
1 x 400g can chopped tomatoes
1 tbsp tomato purée
1 tsp dried oregano
pinch of chilli flakes
1 tsp caster sugar

To serve
400g cooked pasta of your choice
4 tbsp Parmesan cheese, grated
handful of basil leaves, torn

DO THIS STUFF

For the tomato sauce, heat the oil in a large saucepan over a medium heat. Add the onion and cook for 5–7 minutes until just beginning to soften. Add the garlic and cook for a further minute but be careful it does not burn.

Add the tomatoes, tomato purée, oregano, chilli flakes and sugar. Simmer, uncovered, for about 20 minutes or until the sauce thickens slightly. Season and taste adding more sugar or chilli flakes as required.

Meanwhile, mix together the cornflour and turmeric in a shallow bowl. Add the Tofoo and toss until coated well.

Heat the oil in a frying pan over a medium heat and when hot add the Tofoo and fry for 6–7 minutes, turning it to give an even crisp coating.

Add the crispy Tofoo to the tomato sauce and serve with your favourite pasta and a good grating of cheese.

WHY NOT TRY:

· Making the tomato sauce ahead of time. It keeps really well in the fridge for up to five days or can be frozen for a later date.
· For a quick version, use a jar of ready-made tomato pasta sauce.
· Using fresh tomatoes instead of canned for a fresher, sharper flavour.

SMOKED TOFOO
with chimichurri sauce

Chimichurri is a garlicky, herby and tangy sauce, so basically there's nothing it can't improve. In this recipe, the spicy rub enhances the smokiness of the Tofoo and works a treat with the punchy sauce.

Serves: **2**
Preparation: **10 MINUTES**
Marinating: **30 MINUTES**
Cooking: **10 MINUTES**

GET THIS STUFF

1 x 225g pack Smoked Tofoo, drained and dried

For the marinade
1 tsp smoked paprika
1 tsp ground cumin
1 tsp garlic powder
½ tsp ground coriander
2 tsp olive oil

For the chimichurri sauce
30g flat-leaf parsley, chopped
2 garlic cloves, very finely chopped
15g oregano, chopped
1 green chilli, deseeded and finely chopped
80ml extra virgin olive oil
4 tbsp apple cider vinegar
pinch of chilli flakes
½ tsp sea salt

DO THIS STUFF

Add all the chimichurri ingredients to a food processor and blitz until thoroughly combined. Adjust the seasoning to taste and leave to stand for at least 30 minutes before serving. You can do this by hand by finely chopping and mixing all the ingredients together.

For the marinade, mix together the paprika, cumin, garlic powder, ground coriander and oil to make a paste.

Cut the Tofoo in half lengthways to make two 'steaks' about 2cm thick. Spoon the marinade over the Tofoo steaks and press into both sides. Leave to stand for 20 minutes.

Heat a griddle pan until hot. Add the Tofoo steaks and cook for 3–4 minutes or until the steaks can be moved easily. Turn the Tofoo steaks over and cook for a further 3–4 minutes. Cut each Tofoo steak in half to form two triangles.

Serve the Tofoo steaks with a generous helping of the chimichurri sauce. Perfect alongside roasted vegetables and garlic bread.

WHY NOT TRY:

Letting the Tofoo marinate for 30 minutes for a deeper flavour.

SMOKED TOFOO GOULASH

Goulash is a fantastic comfort food. Whip up this easy, hearty dish to feed the family on chilly nights in just 45 minutes.

Serves: **6**
Preparation: **15 MINUTES**
Cooking: **30 MINUTES**

GET THIS STUFF

2 tbsp sunflower oil
1 onion, chopped
2 garlic cloves, crushed
2 tbsp smoked paprika
1 tbsp ground cumin
1 x 225g pack Smoked Tofoo, drained, dried and diced
400g sweet potatoes, peeled and cubed
1 red pepper, deseeded and chopped
1 yellow pepper, deseeded and chopped
2 tbsp tomato purée
1 x 400g can chopped tomatoes
500ml vegetable stock
1 bay leaf
sea salt and freshly ground black pepper

To serve
handful of flat-leaf parsley
coconut yoghurt
cooked basmati rice

DO THIS STUFF

Heat the oil in a large saucepan over a medium heat, add the onion and cook for 4–5 minutes until beginning to soften. Add the garlic and sprinkle with the smoked paprika and cumin. Cook for a few minutes until the onion is soft and golden.

Add the Tofoo, sweet potatoes and peppers to the pan, then stir in the tomato purée.

Add the chopped tomatoes, vegetable stock, 75ml water and the bay leaf. Stir gently to mix all the ingredients. Bring to the boil and cook over a medium heat for 20–25 minutes until the sweet potatoes are soft. Stir every now and again. Season with salt and ground black pepper.

Serve topped with a generous handful of parsley and a dollop of yoghurt alongside boiled rice.

WHY NOT TRY:

Adding chopped chestnut mushrooms for added earthiness.

SUMAC TOFOO STEAKS
with tahini sauce

Sumac is a great spice to have in your storecupboard. Made from dried berries, it has a lemon-lime tartness and is a lovely red-wine colour. If you prepare the pickle, marinate the Tofoo and make the sauce ahead of time, this dish is super speedy to pull together.

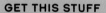

GET THIS STUFF

250g Naked Tofoo, drained, dried and sliced into 4 pieces
2 tbsp sunflower oil

For the marinade
2 tbsp sumac
2 tbsp tamari or lemon juice
3 tbsp ginger paste
2 tsp mild chilli powder
2 tbsp maple syrup
sea salt and freshly ground black pepper

For the tahini sauce
3 tbsp tahini, plus extra to taste
2 tbsp lemon juice
½ tsp garlic powder
¼ tsp sumac, plus extra to taste

DO THIS STUFF

For the cucumber pickle, toss the cucumber with the salt in a colander. Leave for 10 minutes, then squeeze out any excess moisture and pat the ribbons dry with a tea towel. Place the cucumber in a glass jar or bowl.

Mix together the sugar, vinegar, coriander seeds and gingers, and pour over the cucumber ribbons. Refrigerate for a few hours or overnight.

For the tahini sauce, whisk together the tahini, lemon juice and 60ml water in a small bowl. They won't come together straight away, but as you keep stirring. Mix in the garlic powder and sumac. Taste and adjust the seasoning if needed. Keep the sauce in the fridge until ready to serve.

For the Tofoo steaks, mix together the marinade ingredients in a shallow dish. Add the Tofoo steaks and marinate for at least 30 minutes but longer if possible.

Serves: **2**
Preparation: **10 MINUTES**
Marinating: **30 MINUTES**
Cooking: **15 MINUTES**

For the pickled cucumber

1 cucumber, trimmed, cut in half widthways and sliced into ribbons

1 tsp sea salt

2 tbsp caster sugar

5 tbsp white wine vinegar

½ tsp coriander seeds

3cm piece of fresh ginger, peeled and grated

2 stems of ginger in sugar syrup, drained and very finely sliced

Heat the oil in a frying pan over a medium heat. Add the Tofoo and cook for 5–7 minutes, adding any leftover marinade to the pan. Turn the Tofoo over and cook for a further 5 minutes.

Serve two Tofoo steaks per person alongside the tahini sauce and the pickled cucumber.

Delicious with a crisp green salad or pomegranate couscous (see page 90)

WHY NOT TRY:

· Using sumac instead of lemon juice or zest for a twist.
· Adding sumac to cornflour to coat the Tofoo for added sharpness.

TOFOO TIKKA SKEWERS

This skewered version of a favourite curry can be served with rice or in a naan wrap. Remember, if using wooden skewers, you need to soak them for at least 30 minutes to stop them from burning.

Serves: **2**
Preparation: **5 MINUTES**
Marinating: **30+ MINUTES**
Cooking: **10 MINUTES**

GET THIS STUFF

2 tbsp tikka masala paste
2 tbsp natural yoghurt
juice of 1 lemon
250g Naked Tofoo,
   drained, dried and cubed
1 tbsp vegetable oil
sea salt and freshly ground
   black pepper
rice, naan or chapatti,
   to serve

For the yoghurt dip
5 tbsp natural yoghurt
handful of mint leaves,
   finely chopped
¼ cucumber, deseeded
   and very finely chopped

DO THIS STUFF

In a large bowl, mix together the tikka masala paste, yoghurt and lemon juice. Add the Tofoo and mix until well coated. Leave to marinate for at least 30 minutes.

Preheat the grill to high and oil a baking tray or grill pan.

Thread the tikka cubes on to skewers. This is a messy job – be warned! Put the threaded skewers on the tray. Grill for 3–4 minutes on each side until nicely charred.

For the yoghurt dip: mix together the yoghurt, mint and cucumber.

Serve the skewers with rice or wrapped in naan alongside the yoghurt dip.

WHY NOT TRY:

· Adding onion, peppers or even pineapple chunks to the skewers for freshness and sweetness.
· Serving the skewers with a punchy red onion and tomato salad.

RED LENTIL DHAL
with spiced Tofoo

Dhal is one of *the* most comforting of dishes on the planet.
Serving with spiced Tofoo makes it a heartier winter dish.
If you don't have all the spices, just substitute them with
3 teaspoons of garam masala. Easy!

GET THIS STUFF

250g Naked Tofoo,
   drained and dried
4 tsp light soy sauce
2 tsp garam masala

For the dhal
2 tbsp coconut oil
1 onion, finely chopped
3 garlic cloves, finely
   chopped
2cm piece of fresh ginger,
   peeled and grated
1 tsp ground coriander
1 tsp ground cumin
1 tsp ground turmeric
1 tsp garam masala
½ tsp cayenne pepper
300g split red lentils
1 x 400g can chopped
   tomatoes
1 x 400ml can coconut milk
500ml vegetable stock

DO THIS STUFF

For the dhal, heat most of the coconut oil (keeping back about
1 teaspoon) in a large pan over a medium heat and add the onion.
Cook for 5 minutes or until the onion begins to soften. Stir in the
garlic and ginger and cook for a further 1 minute. Add the spices
and stir to combine.

Add the lentils, tomatoes, coconut milk and stock. Bring to the boil,
then reduce the heat and gently simmer for about 20 minutes or until
the lentils are tender. Season well. If you have time, you can leave it to
cook for a little longer over a very low heat, so the flavour develops
further. (Just stir often so it does not catch on the bottom of the pan.)

For the spiced Tofoo, place a frying pan over a medium heat and add
the remaining coconut oil. Add the Tofoo and cook for 5–6 minutes,
tossing the pan often so the Tofoo develops an even golden colour.
Add the soy sauce and garam masala and a pinch of salt. Cook the
Tofoo for a further 3 minutes.

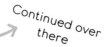

Continued over
there

juice of ½ lemon
100g baby spinach
sea salt and freshly ground
    black pepper

To serve
handful of coriander,
    roughly chopped
naan

Stir in the lemon juice and spinach into the dhal and cook for a couple of minutes until the spinach just wilts.

Serve the dhal topped with the spiced Tofoo and a sprinkling of coriander alongside warm naan.

Image on the next page

WHY NOT TRY:

Freezing the dhal (without the Tofoo) when cooked. Then just defrost, reheat and serve with some freshly cooked Tofoo. Batch cooking win!

RED LENTIL DHAL WITH SPICED TOFOO

KOREAN BARBECUE TOFOO CHUNKS

Gochujang (or red chilli paste) is a savoury, sweet and spicy fermented condiment, popular in Korean cooking. It is now available in most supermarkets or online. Be warned, it's powerful stuff, so use sparingly!

Serves: **4**
Preparation: **15 MINUTES**
Cooking: **15 MINUTES**

GET THIS STUFF

For the Tofoo
2 tbsp cornflour
freshly ground black
    pepper
1 x pack 280g Naked Tofoo,
    drained, dried and torn
    into bite-sized pieces
sunflower oil, for frying

For the spicy Korean sauce
3 tbsp tomato ketchup
1 tbsp gochujang paste
½ tbsp dark soy sauce
1 tbsp maple syrup

To serve
1 small cabbage, stir-fried
2 tbsp white and black
    sesame seeds
2 spring onions, shredded

DO THIS STUFF

For the spicy Korean sauce, combine the ketchup, gochujang, soy sauce and maple syrup in a bowl. Mix well and set aside.

For the Tofoo, season the cornflour with black pepper. Toss the Tofoo cubes in the cornflour, making sure the cornflour gets into all the Tofoo crevices to ensure an extra crispy coating.

Heat 1cm of oil in a frying pan over a medium heat until hot. Add the Tofoo cubes, but do not overcrowd the pan and fry in batches if necessary. Cook on all sides for 7–10 minutes until the Tofoo is golden brown and crispy. Remove and drain on kitchen paper.

Heat the Korean sauce in pan over a low heat, add the Tofoo and stir to coat. Serve piled on stir-fried cabbage and sprinkled with the sesame seeds and spring onions.

WHY NOT TRY:

· Serving with noodles or rice.
· Pairing with delicious kimchi.

TOFOO & CASHEW STIR-FRY

Quick, easy, delicious, adaptable, nutritious – sometimes a good weeknight stir-fry is just unbeatable, and this one is a winner.

Serves: **2**
Preparation: **10 MINUTES**
Cooking: **20 MINUTES**

GET THIS STUFF

150g cashews
250g Naked Tofoo, drained, dried and cut into 1cm-wide strips
3 tbsp cornflour
3–4 tbsp sunflower oil
3 garlic cloves, finely chopped
3 spring onions, sliced
1 red pepper, deseeded and sliced
100g green beans, trimmed and halved
150g sugar snap peas or mangetout, trimmed
noodles or rice, to serve

For the sauce
3 tbsp light soy sauce
1 tbsp rice wine vinegar
1 tsp sesame oil
1½ tsp maple syrup
1 tbsp cornflour
2 tbsp orange juice or water
sea salt and freshly ground black pepper

DO THIS STUFF

Heat a wok or heavy-based pan over a medium heat. Add the cashews and dry-fry for 10 minutes or until they begin to turn golden brown. You will need to keep an eye on them as they can burn easily.

Break each Tofoo strip into 3–4 chunks. Dry each chunk really well with kitchen paper. Drying and breaking the Tofoo makes it even crispier.

Place the chunks into a bowl with the cornflour. Toss well so all the edges of the Tofoo are fully coated.

Heat 2 tablespoons of oil in the wok or frying pan over medium-high heat. Add the Tofoo and fry for 6–7 minutes, flipping occasionally, until golden brown and crispy. Do not overcrowd the pan or the Tofoo will not get crispy. Remove from the pan and drain on kitchen paper.

Wipe the pan and heat 2 tablespoons of oil. Add the garlic, spring onions and red pepper, and stir-fry for 1–2 minutes. Add the green beans and sugar snap peas. Return the Tofoo and cashews to the pan.

For the sauce, mix together the soy sauce, rice wine vinegar, sesame oil and maple syrup in a small bowl. Mix together the cornflour and orange juice and stir into the sauce. Add the sauce to the Tofoo and vegetables and stir to coat. Cook for a couple of minutes until the sauce is thick and glossy.

Serve with a side of noodles or rice.

BLACK PEPPER TOFOO

Quick, easy and fiery. But how fiery? You decide! Play around with the amount of chilli and black pepper until you find the perfect balance.

Serves: **2**
Preparation: **5 MINUTES**
Cooking: **25 MINUTES**

GET THIS STUFF

- 250g Naked Tofoo, drained, dried and cut into 2 cubes
- 1 tsp Chinese 5 spice
- 3 tbsp cornflour
- vegetable oil, for frying
- 6 shallots, finely sliced
- 2 red chillies, deseeded and sliced
- 3 garlic cloves, crushed
- 3cm piece of fresh ginger, peeled and finely chopped
- 6 tbsp light soy sauce
- 3 tbsp sweet chilli sauce
- 2 tbsp light brown sugar
- 3 tbsp coarsely crushed black peppercorns
- stir-fried pak choi and Tenderstem broccoli, to serve

DO THIS STUFF

Dry the Tofoo really well with kitchen paper. Mix the Chinese 5 spice with the cornflour. Toss the Tofoo in the spiced cornflour, shaking off any excess.

Heat 4 tablespoons of vegetable oil in a deep frying pan over a medium heat until hot. Add the Tofoo and cook, turning the cubes over in the oil for 10–12 minutes until golden and crispy all over. You may need to do this in batches. Once cooked, transfer the crispy Tofoo on to kitchen paper.

Drain the oil and any sediments from the pan. Pour 2 tablespoons of oil back into the pan and heat over a medium heat, then add the shallots, chillies, garlic and ginger. Cook over a low heat for about 15 minutes or until the onions are soft and sticky. Add the soy sauce, chilli sauce and the black pepper. The sauce should become dark and sticky.

Add the Tofoo and cover in the sauce. Serve with stir-fried pak choi and Tenderstem broccoli.

WHY NOT TRY:

- Serving with green beans and mangetout.
- Making the sauce ahead and then when ready to serve, adding the crispy Tofoo and vegetables.

TOFOO PAELLA

A smoky paella golden in colour and bursting with flavour.
Ideally enjoyed on a terrace under the sun in Spain, but
also great in your kitchen any time of year.

GET THIS STUFF

large pinch of saffron
   strands
600ml good quality
   vegetable stock
3 tbsp olive oil, plus extra
   for drizzling
1 x 280g pack Naked
   Tofoo, drained, dried
   and cut into 3cm cubes
1 tsp smoked paprika
1 onion, finely chopped
3 garlic cloves, finely
   chopped
1 red pepper, deseeded
   and chopped
1 courgette, chopped
2 tsp smoked paprika
250g paella rice
450ml boiling water
4 medium tomatoes,
   roughly chopped
1 x 210g can chickpeas,
   drained and rinsed
75g frozen peas
sea salt and freshly ground
   black pepper

DO THIS STUFF

Stir the saffron strands into the stock and set aside to infuse while
starting to make the paella.

Heat 2 tablespoons of oil in a paella pan or a large, deep frying pan
with a lid over a medium heat. Add the Tofoo, and half the smoked
paprika. Toss and fry for about 3 minutes until crisp and the oil
has been released. Remove the Tofoo and drain on kitchen paper,
leaving the oil in the pan.

Return the pan to the heat, stir in the onion and fry for 4–5 minutes
until softened and just starting to colour. Stir in the garlic, red
pepper, courgette and remaining smoked paprika with the
remaining tablespoon of oil. Fry for a further 1–2 minutes.

To serve
small handful of flat-leaf
    parsley, chopped
lemon wedges

Add the rice and stir so it is well coated in the oil, pour in the saffron-infused stock plus the boiling water, scraping up the sticky brown bits from the bottom of the pan with a wooden spoon. Stir in the chopped tomatoes, season, cover and cook over a medium heat for 10 minutes, stirring occasionally. Scatter the chickpeas, peas and Tofoo over the top. Cover again and leave to cook for a further 5–10 minutes, or until the rice is just cooked and most of the liquid in the pan has been absorbed.

Remove the pan from the heat, cover and leave to stand for 5 minutes. Scatter over the chopped parsley. Serve with lemon wedges.

Image on the next page

WHY NOT TRY:

- Adding chorizo for an even more authentic flavour.
- Green olives can add a salty element to this delicious paella.

TOFOO PAELLA

ZA'ATAR-SPICED TOFOO

Typically, za'atar is a blend of dried thyme, oregano, marjoram, sumac, toasted sesame seeds and salt, but there are many variations, and you can make your own or buy it ready-made. Sprinkle over dips or rice or add to dressings. It is a great ingredient to have in the ol' storecupboard, so stock up!

GET THIS STUFF

For the za'atar-spiced Tofoo
juice of 1 lemon
2 tsp maple syrup
1 tbsp light soy sauce
3 tbsp za'atar
2 tbsp olive oil, plus extra for greasing
1 x 280g pack Naked Tofoo, drained, dried and cut into 2cm strips
freshly ground black pepper
tomato and cucumber salad, to serve

For the flatbreads
200g plain flour, plus extra for dusting
200g Greek yoghurt

DO THIS STUFF

Combine the lemon juice, maple syrup, soy sauce, za'atar and oil in a small bowl.

In a shallow bowl, lay out the Tofoo strips and pour over the za'atar marinade. Leave to marinate for at least 30 minutes, flipping the Tofoo to ensure an even covering. For even better results, marinate overnight.

When ready to cook, preheat the oven to 200°C/180°C fan/400°F/gas mark 6. Line a baking sheet with baking paper.

Lay the Tofoo on the prepared baking sheet. Season with black pepper. Cook for 20–25 minutes, turning over the Tofoo after 10 minutes and basting with the marinade. Cook until the Tofoo is beginning to turn golden brown.

While the Tofoo is cooking, make the flatbreads. Place the flour in a mixing bowl and add the yoghurt. Stir to combine until the dough starts to form into a ball. Tip the dough on to a well-floured surface and knead with your hands for a minute or two. If the dough is still too sticky, add some more flour and continue to knead.

Or make eight small balls for mini flatbreads

For the dill sauce
150g Greek yoghurt
3 garlic cloves, crushed
2 tbsp dill, chopped
2 tbsp lemon juice
a drizzle of olive oil

Divide the dough into four balls and set aside for at least 15 minutes.

Lightly grease a work surface with olive oil, then use a rolling pin to roll each ball of dough into a disc about the size of your frying pan.

Heat the frying pan over medium heat. Once the pan is hot, add a flatbread and cook on each side for 20–30 seconds until cooked through and covered in brown spots. Repeat with the remaining flatbreads.

For the dill yoghurt: add the yoghurt, garlic, dill, salt, lemon juice and olive oil to a small mixing bowl and stir to combine.

Serve the flatbreads topped with the za'atar-spiced Tofoo and a drizzle of the dill yoghurt.

WHY NOT TRY:

· Making the Tofoo into skewers and serving in wraps.
· Serving the Tofoo with ready-made hummus.

CITRUS TOFOO TRAYBAKE
with pesto beans

This fresh citrus Tofoo traybake is easy, fuss-free and deliciously nutritious. You can make it even easier by using shop-bought pesto. We won't tell if you don't!

Serves: **4**
Preparation: **10 MINUTES**
Cooking: **35 MINUTES**

GET THIS STUFF

2 x 280g packs Naked Tofoo, drained, dried and each block halved
175ml orange juice
2 tbsp orange zest
2 tbsp light soy sauce
2 tbsp maple syrup
1 tbsp coconut oil
½ tsp white wine vinegar
2 tsp cornflour mixed with 1 tbsp water
watercress, to serve

For the pesto beans
1 x 400g can cannellini beans, drained and rinsed
2 tbsp kale pesto (see page 189)
1 tsp nutritional yeast
4 tbsp pine nuts, toasted
sea salt and freshly ground black pepper

DO THIS STUFF

Preheat the oven to 200°C/180°C fan/400°F/gas mark 6. Line a baking sheet with baking paper.

Sit the Tofoo slices on the prepared baking sheet.

Mix the orange juice and zest with the soy sauce, maple syrup, coconut oil and vinegar in a small pan. Heat over a medium heat for about 3 minutes or until combined. Add the cornflour mixture and heat for a further 2–3 minutes, stirring regularly, until the sauce thickens.

Reserve roughly a quarter of the orange sauce to pour over the Tofoo after baking. Pour the remaining orange sauce over the Tofoo rectangles, then flip the Tofoo to coat it evenly with the sauce.

Bake the Tofoo for 10 minutes, then flip the Tofoo over and bake for a further 10–15 minutes or until golden brown. Keep an eye on it to make sure it doesn't get too dark; it should just caramelise.

Once the Tofoo is golden brown, remove from the oven and glaze with the reserved orange sauce.

Mix together the beans, pesto, nutritional yeast and season. Stir to combine. Taste and adjust the seasoning to taste.

Top each Tofoo slice with spoonful of the pesto beans, pine nuts and a handful of watercress.

TOFOO FRIED RICE

You worked late, and now you're very hungry and not very patient. We understand. This dish will be ready in no time and uses handy storecupboard ingredients for a dinner in minutes.

Serves: **2**
Preparation: **10 MINUTES**
Cooking: **15 MINUTES**

GET THIS STUFF

250g Naked Tofoo, drained, dried and crumbled
½ tsp ground turmeric
2 tbsp sunflower oil
1 red pepper, deseeded and finely chopped
1 green pepper, deseeded and finely chopped
100g frozen peas
4 spring onions, sliced
1 x 250g pack microwave basmati rice
2 tbsp light soy sauce
2 tsp oyster sauce
½ tsp toasted sesame oil, plus extra to drizzle
sea salt and freshly ground black pepper

DO THIS STUFF

Dry the Tofoo with kitchen paper and toss in a bowl with the turmeric.

Heat a wok or large frying pan with the oil over a medium heat and add the peppers. Stir-fry for 3–4 minutes or until the peppers start to soften. Add the peas, spring onions and the rice. Stir to break up the rice and avoid any clumps. Season with salt and pepper and stir-fry for about 5 minutes.

Add the turmeric Tofoo and stir-fry for 5 minutes until the Tofoo turns bright yellow.

Stir together the soy sauce, oyster sauce and sesame oil, and pour over the rice.

Stir-fry to combine.

Serve in bowls, drizzled with a little sesame oil.

WHY NOT TRY:

· Using leftover vegetables, such as carrots or butternut squash.
· Scattering with a handful of chopped flat-leaf parsley or coriander to give the dish some freshness.

TOFOO WITH KALE PESTO PASTA

Pesto pasta, but better. This vibrant pesto recipe is nutty, bright and delicious.

Serves: **4**
Preparation: **30 MINUTES**
Cooking: **10 MINUTES**

GET THIS STUFF

1 tbsp olive oil
1 x 280g pack Naked
   Tofoo, drained, dried
   and cut into 2cm cubes
300g of pasta of your
   choice

For the pesto*
100g kale or cavolo nero,
   stems removed and
   leaves roughly chopped
50g basil leaves
1 tbsp capers, rinsed
4 tbsp extra virgin olive oil
20g pine nuts, toasted
2 garlic cloves, chopped
zest and juice of 1 lemon
30g Parmesan cheese,
   grated, plus extra for
   serving
sea salt and freshly ground
   black pepper

DO THIS STUFF

Bring a large pan of water to the boil and add the kale or cavolo nero. Blanch for 5 minutes until just tender. Drain and add to a food processor along with the remaining pesto ingredients and whizz until smooth. Scrape down the sides of the processor and whizz once more to thoroughly combine. Season.

Heat the oil in a frying pan over a medium heat and when hot, add the Tofoo and cook for 2–3 minutes on each side until golden and crispy. Remove the Tofoo and drain on kitchen paper, then season well.

Cook the pasta following the pack instructions. Drain, return to the pan and add the Tofoo and kale pesto. Toss to cover. Serve topped with a good grating of cheese.

* If you want a quick easy version of this dish, you can use shop-bought pesto

WHY NOT TRY:

Swapping the pine nuts for walnuts or hazelnuts.

LOADED SPICY TOFOO NACHOS

Perfect for sharing, these nachos are best served with salsa and guacamole and totally covered in melted cheese. Ideal for a film night and for sharing with friends.

Serves: **4**
Preparation: **10 MINUTES**
Cooking: **10 MINUTES**

GET THIS STUFF

2 tbsp sunflower oil
1 x 225g pack Smoked Tofoo, drained, ripped into chunks and dried
1 tbsp Cajun spice mix
3 tsp pickled jalapeños, chopped, plus extra to serve
1 small red onion, finely chopped
2 large ripe tomatoes, finely chopped
juice of 2 limes, plus wedges to serve
30g coriander, finely chopped, plus a few leaves to serve
2 ripe avocados
1 x 180g pack salted tortilla chips
1 x 325g can sweetcorn, drained
250g mature Cheddar cheese, grated
sea salt and freshly ground black pepper

DO THIS STUFF

Preheat the oven to 200°C/180°C fan/400°F/gas mark 6.

Pour the oil into a small bowl and add the Tofoo, Cajun spice mix and 1 teaspoon of jalapeños. Toss gently.

Heat a frying pan over a medium heat, add the Tofoo mix and fry for 7–10 minutes or until the Tofoo is beginning to crisp. Remove the Tofoo and drain on kitchen paper.

Mix the onion, tomatoes, remaining jalapeños, half the lime juice and the chopped coriander in a bowl.

Mash the avocados with 1 tablespoon of lime juice to make guacamole. Season and add more lime juice to suit your taste.

In a shallow ovenproof dish, layer the tortilla chips and top with Tofoo, half the onion mix and the sweetcorn. Sprinkle over the cheese, ensuring that most of the tortilla chips on top are covered with cheese. Bake for 8–10 minutes until toasted and the cheese is bubbling.

Spoon over dollops of the remaining onion mix, guacamole, extra coriander and pickled jalapeños.

WHY NOT TRY:

· Adding a layer of refried beans to the nachos.
· Sprinkling the layers with a chopped red chilli.

CRISPY TOFOO UDON BOWL

Udon is an incredible moreish noodle dish, and the addition of crispy Tofoo is a great way to sneak some protein in.

GET THIS STUFF

100ml dark soy sauce
1 tsp toasted sesame oil
½ tsp honey or maple syrup
1 x 280g pack Naked Tofoo, drained, dried and cut into 2cm cubes
½ tsp cornflour
1 x 200g pack ready-to-wok udon noodles
2cm piece of fresh ginger, peeled and finely chopped
1 small carrot, peeled and diced
2 baby pak choi, chopped
¼ red cabbage, finely shredded

DO THIS STUFF

Preheat the oven to 200°C/180°C fan/400°F/gas mark 6. Line a baking tray with baking paper.

In a bowl, mix together the soy sauce, half the sesame oil and the honey or maple syrup.

Add a third of the soy mixture to a bowl with the Tofoo, mix completely, then add the cornflour. Mix until you don't see any more cornflour. The Tofoo should look almost dry and not wet from the sauce.

Place Tofoo on the prepared baking sheet. Bake for 30 minutes, turning every 5–7 minutes so each side gets a chance to crisp up to a deep golden brown.

Fill a small pan with water and bring to the boil. Add the noodles and use a chopstick to gently unstick the noodles.

Add the remaining sesame oil to a large pan over a medium heat. Add the ginger and carrot and cook for about 5 minutes, stirring occasionally. Add the pak choi and Tofoo. Reduce the heat and stir.

Serves: **4**

Preparation: **20 MINUTES**

Cooking: **35 MINUTES**

To serve

handful of coriander
  leaves, torn

2 spring onions, sliced

2 tbsp sesame seeds

Once the noodles are completely loose, use tongs to remove them from the pan, and add them to the pan with the Tofoo. Pour in the remaining soy sauce mixture and add the red cabbage. Mix well until the noodles are completely coated in the sauce.

Serve with a scattering of coriander, spring onions and sesame seeds.

Image on the
next page

 WHY NOT TRY:

- Adding some hot sauce or sriracha to the soy mixture for an added kick to the dish.
- Stirring in a handful of cooked edamame beans.

5

A Bit on the Side

TOFOO CAJUN FRIES

You can buy ready-made Cajun spice mix in most supermarkets but making your own means you can alter it to suit your taste, so get mixing!

Serves: **2**
Preparation: **5 MINUTES**
Cooking: **5 MINUTES**

GET THIS STUFF

2 tbsp Cajun spice mix
1 tsp sea salt
100g cornflour
1 x 280g pack Naked
  Tofoo, drained, dried
  and cut into 1cm batons
sunflower oil, for frying
dips of your choice,
  to serve

We like ours with tomato salsa and herby mayo

DO THIS STUFF

Dry each Tofoo baton really well with kitchen paper.

Mix the Cajun spice mix and salt together with the cornflour. Add the Tofoo batons and toss until well coated.

Add about 5mm of sunflower oil to a frying pan over a medium heat. Add the Tofoo and cook for 2–3 minutes turning over until golden brown on all sides.

Serve the Tofoo fries in a bowl alongside dips of your choice.

WHY NOT TRY:

A slightly different coating by mixing the cornflour with one of the following:
- freshly chopped rosemary and garlic powder
- smoked paprika
- sumac
- curry powder

TOFOO HALLOUMI

This recipe is a vegan take on everyone's favourite squeaky cheese. Serve in a salad or as part of a mezze. It may not squeak like the real stuff, but it's just as tasty.

Serves: **2**
Preparation: **10 MINUTES**
Marinating: **30 MINUTES**
Cooking: **10 MINUTES**

GET THIS STUFF

1 x 280g pack Naked Tofoo, drained, dried and cut into 0.5cm slices

For the marinade
juice of 1 lemon
2 tsp sea salt flakes
4 tbsp nutritional yeast
1 tbsp dried mint
2 tbsp olive oil
sprinkle of black pepper

DO THIS STUFF

Mix together all the marinade ingredients in a shallow bowl.

Lay out Tofoo and rub a little marinade into both sides of each slice. Set aside for 5 minutes.

Place the Tofoo into the remaining marinade and leave to marinate for a further 30 minutes.

Preheat a griddle pan until medium hot. Griddle the Tofoo for 8–10 minutes until golden and slightly charred, turning over once.

Serve as part of a salad or alongside a dip.

WHY NOT TRY:

· Swapping the dried mint for dried oregano.
· Marinating for up to 12 hours for a full-flavoured 'halloumi'.

TOFOO & VEGETABLE FRITTERS

You can be fairly flexible with which vegetables you use for these fritters – consider carrots, parsnips, spring onions, peppers or broccoli. Serve with Tofoo bacon (see page 21) for a delicious brunch dish.

Serves: **2** as a main course or **4** as a starter
Preparation: **15 MINUTES**
Cooking: **20 MINUTES**

1 courgette, grated
1 x 200g can sweetcorn, drained
1 red onion, chopped
½ x 225g pack Smoked Tofoo, drained, dried and crumbled
100g chickpea flour (gram flour)
½ tsp paprika
½ tsp ground cumin
½ tsp garlic powder
2 tsp dried mint
150ml milk of your choice
2 tbsp light soy sauce
2–4 tbsp sunflower oil
sea salt and freshly ground black pepper
yoghurt and mint dip, to serve

Place the courgette in a colander and dry with kitchen paper to remove as much of the moisture as possible. Once dry, place in a large bowl.

Add the sweetcorn, onion and crumbled Tofoo to the courgette.

In a separate bowl, mix together the chickpea flour, spices and mint. Season and mix again.

Pour in the milk and soy sauce and whisk to form a thick batter. Add the batter to the vegetable mixture and stir together. It should be dropping consistency.

Heat 3 tbsp of oil in a frying pan over a medium heat. Drop about 1 tablespoon of batter into the frying pan and cook each fritter for 7–8 minutes on each side until golden brown. You will probably fit about 2–3 fritters in the pan at once, but make sure you do not overcrowd the pan. Continue cooking, adding more oil if necessary, until you have used up all the batter; you should have about eight fritters.

Serve these as close as you can to making them as they really benefit from being eaten nice and crisp, straight from the pan. Delicious served with a yoghurt and mint dip.

WHY NOT TRY:

Adding finely chopped red pepper to the fritter mix.

TOFETA

Make a batch of Tofeta every week and you will never have to wonder what's for lunch ever again! Add a sprinkle to salads, crumbled on to wraps or into a shakshuka.

Serves: **4**

Preparation: **5 MINUTES**

Marinating: **2 HOURS**

GET THIS STUFF

1 x 280g pack Naked Tofoo, drained, dried and cut into 2cm cubes

For the marinade
2 tbsp white miso paste
juice of 1 lemon
3 tbsp cider vinegar
1 tbsp olive oil
2 tbsp nutritional yeast
1 tbsp dried oregano
½ tsp garlic powder
½ tsp salt
freshly ground black pepper
pinch of chilli flakes (optional)

DO THIS STUFF

Whisk all the marinade ingredients together with 3 tablespoons of water. Add the Tofoo cubes and toss to coat. Leave to marinate in the fridge for 2 hours or preferably overnight.

After marinating, keep the Tofoo in an airtight jar covered with olive oil in the fridge to preserve it for 2–3 weeks.

We think Tofeta is even better than feta!

WHY NOT TRY:

Adding fresh herbs, chilli, black peppercorns and garlic cloves for an extra zingy version.

MINI TOFOO & CRANBERRY ROLLS

Whether it's for a snack, or part of a grazing lunch or picnic, there is something simple and comforting about a good old 'sausage' roll. The cranberry gives these rolls a fruity touch that works wonders.

GET THIS STUFF

1 tbsp olive oil
1 onion, diced
1 x 280g pack Naked Tofoo, drained, dried and roughly cubed
120g fresh white breadcrumbs (about 3 slices of bread)
3 tsp dried sage
1 tsp dried thyme
100ml sherry
1 tbsp cornflour
50g dried cranberries
1 tbsp maple syrup
2 tbsp soya or almond milk
plain flour, for dusting
1 x 375g ready-rolled puff pastry
tomato chutney or cranberry sauce, for dipping

DO THIS STUFF

Heat the oil in a frying pan over a medium heat and fry the onion for 5 minutes until just softened. Leave to cool slightly.

Place the Tofoo, breadcrumbs, sage, thyme, sherry, cornflour and cooked onions in a food processor. Add the dried cranberries and whizz until well combined.

Mix together the maple syrup and milk to make a glaze.

Preheat the oven to 200°C/180°C fan/400°F/gas mark 6.

Unroll the pastry on a lightly floured board and roll out until 2mm thick, then cut in half lengthways.

Divide the Tofoo mixture in two and spread along the length of each pastry strip in a cylinder shape, leaving a 1cm border.

Brush the glaze along the long edges of the pastry, then fold one side over the filling, pressing to prevent any air bubbles, then fold over the other side sealing the pastry. Roll the long sausage over so that the seam of the pastry is on the bottom. Cut each length into six rolls. Make two little slashes in the top of each roll with a knife.

Place on a baking tray, then brush the top of each roll with the glaze and bake for 25–30 minutes until golden brown.

Serve with a tomato chutney or cranberry sauce dip.

Image on the next page

WHY NOT TRY:

- Adding chopped cooked mushrooms to the filling.
- Spicing up the filling with a pinch of chilli flakes.
- Brushing the pastry with a little mustard before adding the filling.

TOFOO TEMPURA

A light crispy batter that complements the soft Tofoo centre perfectly. Consider us sold. Serve with sharp pickled vegetables as a delicious starter.

Serves: **2** as a main course or **4** as a starter
Preparation: **15 MINUTES**
Cooking: **20 MINUTES**

GET THIS STUFF

1 x 225g pack Smoked Tofoo, drained, dried and ripped into 8 pieces
120g plain flour
2 tbsp cornflour
1 tbsp baking powder
½ tsp sea salt
freshly ground black pepper
250ml sparkling water or beer
500ml vegetable oil
pickled vegetables, to serve

See pickled onion, page 48

DO THIS STUFF

Dry the Tofoo well with kitchen paper. The drier the Tofoo the crispier the batter.

Mix together the flour, cornflour, baking powder, salt and some pepper in a large bowl.

Slowly whisk in the sparkling water or beer until well combined, but don't overmix. Set aside.

Pour the oil into a large saucepan, and heat gently to a temperature of 170°C/325°F. If you do not have a thermometer, test the oil by dropping in a piece of tempura. If the tempura drops to the bottom but comes up right after that, the oil is at the correct temperature. If the tempura does not drop to the bottom at all, the oil is too hot.

Dip the Tofoo pieces into the batter, one at a time, to lightly coat, shaking off any excess batter. Fry two or three pieces at a time for 1–2 minutes, then flip to ensure even cooking and cook for a further 1–2 minutes. Do not overcrowd the pan.

Serve with pickled vegetables.

WHY NOT TRY:

· Cooking in a deep-fat fryer.
· Serving with a hot chilli or soy sauce dip.

CRISPY TOFOO CRUMB

Use this flavour-packed crumb to sprinkle on salads, mac 'n' cheese, soups or bakes for a little extra something.

Preparation: **15 MINUTES**
Cooking: **30 MINUTES**

GET THIS STUFF

1 x 225g pack Smoked Tofoo, drained and dried
1 tbsp vegetable oil
1 tbsp light soy sauce
2 tsp mild chilli powder
½ tsp garlic powder

DO THIS STUFF

Preheat the oven to 200°C/180°C fan/400°F/gas mark 6.

Using the large side of a cheese grater, grate the block of Tofoo into shreds. Dry with kitchen paper and set aside.

Mix the oil, soy sauce, chilli powder and garlic powder in a large bowl. Add the shredded Tofoo and use a spatula to gently toss and evenly coat the Tofoo in the seasoning.

Spread the Tofoo evenly over a baking tray. Bake for 25–30 minutes, stirring the Tofoo halfway through cooking, until browned. For chewier shreds, bake for a further 5 minutes, or for more tender shreds, reduce the cooking time to 20 minutes.

WHY NOT TRY:

- Breaking the Tofoo into crumbs, cooking as above and eating as a snack.
- Adding chilli flakes or smoked paprika.

THIN TOFOO CRISPS

A delicious, healthier alternative to crisps – and you can choose your own flavourings.

Serves: **2-4**
Preparation: **10 MINUTES**
Cooking: **25 MINUTES**

GET THIS STUFF

1 x 280g pack Naked Tofoo, drained and dried
2–3 tbsp olive oil
1–2 tbsp dark soy sauce
2 tsp sea salt
1 tsp paprika
1 tsp ground cumin
1 tsp ground coriander

Perfect for dipping in salsa!

DO THIS STUFF

Preheat the oven to 220°C/200°C fan/425°F/gas mark 7. Line a baking sheet with foil.

Cut the block of Tofoo into slices as thin as you can get without them falling apart (about 5mm is fine). Place the slices on sheets of kitchen paper to absorb any excess moisture.

Place the Tofoo slices on the prepared baking sheet. Very lightly brush the slices with oil. Sprinkle each slice with soy sauce and a generous sprinkling of salt.

Bake, checking every 5–7 minutes or so. When the pieces are starting to look golden brown around the edges, remove the tray and flip them over. Rearrange the slices so that the more well done ones are exchanged with the paler, less crispy ones to get a consistent crunch.

Cook for a further 5–7 minutes or until golden brown. Once cooked, move the slices on to a wire rack, or plate lined with kitchen paper. If you can leave to cool and enjoy as a snack. Keep in a sealed container for 2–3 days.

WHY NOT TRY:

· Sprinkling with flavoured salt, such as roasted garlic sea salt or chilli salt.
· Scattering over za'atar or sumac just after baking.

BAKED BUFFALO TOFOO

Delicious simple, moreish – these crispy baked buffalo Tofoo wings make the perfect appetiser at a party or are great added to a salad!

Serves: **2-4**
Preparation: **10 MINUTES**
Cooking: **35 MINUTES**

2 tbsp cornflour
2 tbsp smoked paprika
1 tbsp ground cumin
1 tbsp sea salt
1 tbsp dark brown sugar
1 x 225g pack Smoked Tofoo, drained, dried and ripped into bite-sized pieces

For the buffalo sauce
125ml hot sauce
75g butter
1 tbsp apple cider vinegar
1 tbsp maple syrup

Preheat the oven to 200°C/180°C fan/400°F/gas mark 6.

Mix together the cornflour, smoked paprika, cumin, sea salt and sugar. Dry the Tofoo really well with kitchen paper. Add to the cornflour mix and toss until well coated. Lay the Tofoo on a baking tray and bake for 15 minutes, then flip the Tofoo pieces and bake for a further 10 minutes.

Place all the buffalo sauce ingredients in a saucepan over a medium heat and simmer for 5 minutes, then remove from the heat.

Tip the baked Tofoo into a large bowl and cover with buffalo sauce. Return the Tofoo to the baking sheet and bake for a further 10 minutes. Serve as a snack or as a starter. Yum!

WHY NOT TRY:

· Adding garlic powder to the buffalo sauce.
· Frying the Tofoo instead of baking for added crunch.

CRISPY TOFOO NUGGETS

A great snack to have on film night. Serve in a paper cone in front of a classic movie for the authentic experience.

Serves: **2-4**
Preparation: **10 MINUTES**
Cooking: **10 MINUTES**

GET THIS STUFF

150ml soya milk
75g plain flour
2 tsp garlic powder
2 tsp hot paprika
100g panko breadcrumbs
1 x 280g pack Naked Tofoo, drained, dried and cut into 2cm cubes
vegetable oil, for frying
cayenne pepper (optional)
sea salt and freshly ground black pepper
garlic mayonnaise or ketchup, to serve

DO THIS STUFF

Whisk together the soya milk, flour, garlic powder and paprika, and season with plenty of salt and pepper.

Spread the panko breadcrumbs over a plate. Dry the Tofoo cubes really well. Working in batches, coat the Tofoo in the soya milk mixture, then toss in the panko breadcrumbs to coat completely.

Heat 2cm of oil in a large, deep frying pan over a medium heat. Fry the Tofoo in batches until golden and crisp. This should only take about 1–2 minutes per batch. Remove from the oil using a slotted spoon and place on a baking tray lined with kitchen paper.

Sprinkle with a little salt and cayenne pepper, if using, before digging in and dipping into garlic mayonnaise or ketchup.

WHY NOT TRY:

- Marinating the Tofoo squares in soy or hot sauce before crumbing for a saltier chilli bite.
- Using breadcrumbs or even crushed cornflakes rather than panko breadcrumbs.
- Serving these nuggets with chips or potato wedges.

YAKITORI-STYLE TOFOO SKEWERS

Easy-to-make grilled skewers, marinated in a traditional Japanese sauce mixture of mirin, sake and tamari. Perfect for a fresh take on summer barbecue food.

Serves: **4-6** as a starter or canapé

Preparation: **10 MINUTES**

Marinating: **2 HOURS**

Cooking: **20 MINUTES**

GET THIS STUFF

1 x 280g pack Naked Tofoo, drained, dried and cut into 12 cubes

4 spring onions

1 tbsp sesame seeds

For the yakitori marinade

3 tbsp maple syrup

3 tbsp dark soy sauce

juice of 3 limes

3 tsp toasted sesame oil

DO THIS STUFF

To make the yakitori marinade, whisk together all the ingredients in a small pan over a medium heat. Cook for 3–5 minutes or until the sauce thickens and reduces by half. Do not turn your back on this sauce as it can burn very easily. Leave to cool slightly, then add the Tofoo and leave for at least 2 hours.

Preheat the grill to medium. Line a baking sheet with foil.

To make spring onions curl, thinly slice the spring onions lengthways. Submerge in a bowl of cold water and chill in the fridge until ready to serve.

Sit the Tofoo cubes on the prepared baking sheet and grill for 12 minutes. Turn each square over regulary. As you grill, the sauce gets stickier, so use the Tofoo squares to mop up the sticky sauce on the baking sheet. Cook by basting the squares each time you turn them over, until you have a golden brown, sticky Tofoo cubes.

Spear each Tofoo cube with a short cocktail stick, then sprinkle with sesame seeds and a few spring onion curls to serve.

Image on the next page

WHY NOT TRY:

Threading a few cubes on a skewer and serving as a starter.

YAKITORI-STYLE TOFOO SKEWERS

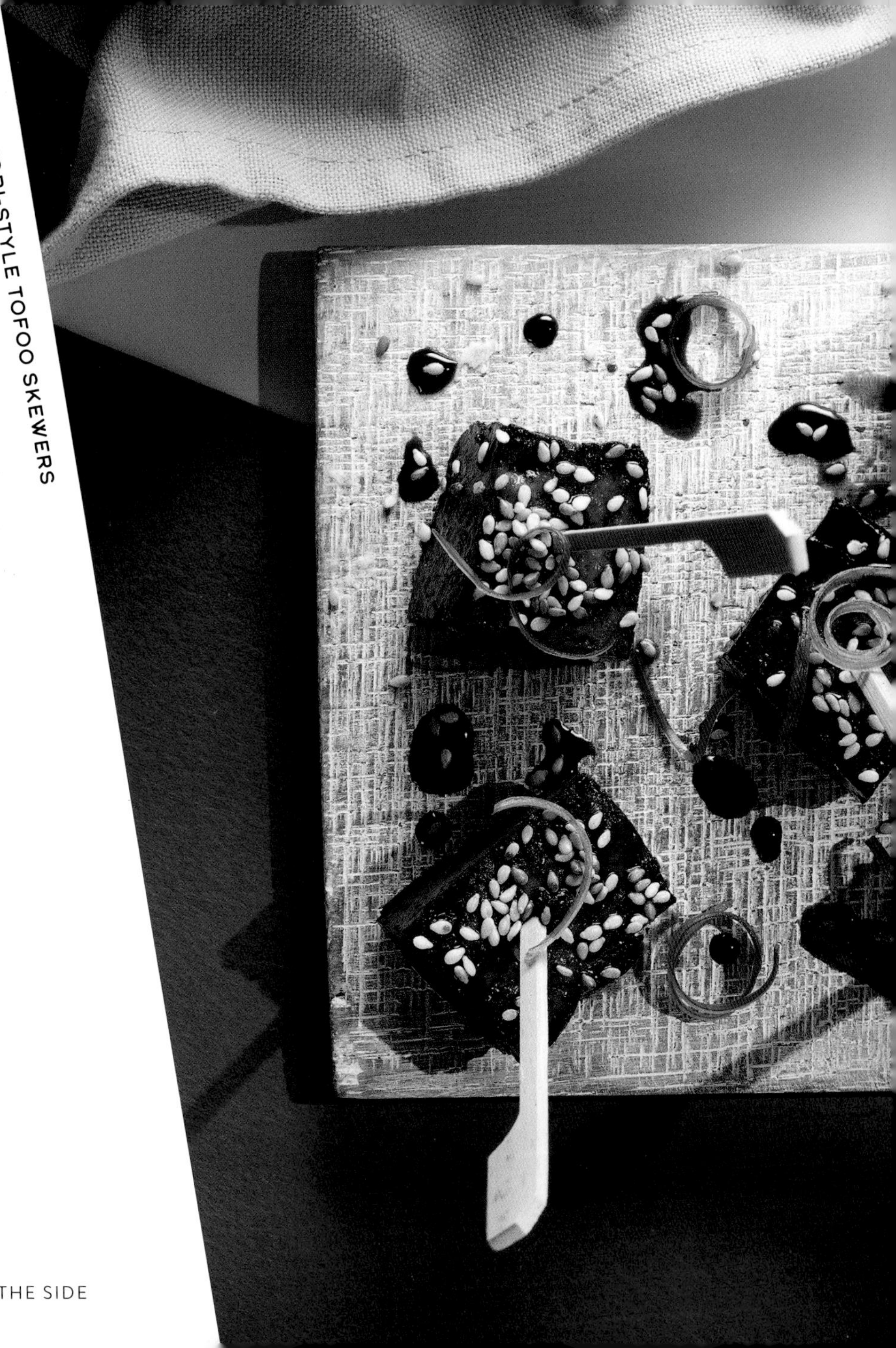

INDEX

Published in 2022 by Ebury Press an imprint of Ebury Publishing,
20 Vauxhall Bridge Road,
London SW1V 2SA

Ebury Press is part of the Penguin Random House group of companies
whose addresses can be found at global.penguinrandomhouse.com

Writer: Mari Williams
Prop Stylist: Rachel Vere
Food Stylist: Mari Williams
Production: Sian Pratley
Editor: Camilla Ackley

All recipes by Mari Williams except:
Robert Barker: p.8, 21, 23, 32, 33, 43, 112, 116, 140
Samantha Wilson: p.120, 122, 123, 130, 134
Tanya Sadourian: p. 16, 114, 118
Sian Davies: p.162, 166
Jeremy Pang: p.89

This edition first published by Ebury Press in 2022

www.penguin.co.uk

A CIP catalogue record for this book is available from the British Library

ISBN 9781529148527

Printed and bound in Slovakia by TBB.as